A TREASURY
OF CHRISTMAS

A TREASURY OF CHRISTMAS

FRANK & JAMIE MUIR

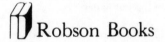

Robson Books

Acknowledgments

Photographs and illustrations were supplied by or are reproduced by kind permission of the following: The Earl of Pembroke at Wilton House, Wiltshire; The Trustees of the Chatsworth Settlement; Arts Council of Great Britain; British Museum; Cooper Bridgeman Library; Giraudon; George Hoare, Drury Lane; Angelo Hornak; London Library; Mansell Collection; Mary Evans Picture Library; Musée Condé, Chantilly; National Galleries of Scotland; National Monuments Record; Raymond Mander and Joe Mitchenson Theatre Collection; Scala; Sotheby Parke Bernet Publications; Victoria and Albert Museum; Welsh Folk Museum.

Poems are reproduced by kind permission of the following: *Christmas* by John Betjeman from *Collected Poems:* John Murray (Publishers) Ltd; *Well, So That is That* by W. H. Auden from *Collected Longer Poems:* Faber and Faber Ltd; *Journey of the Magi* by T. S. Eliot from *Collected Poems 1909-1962:* Faber and Faber Ltd.

Picture Research Philippa Lewis

Designed by Paul Turner

First published in Great Britain in 1981 by Robson Books Ltd, Bolsover House, 5–6 Clipstone Street, London W1P 7EB
This Robson paperback edition first published 1991

British Library Cataloguing in Publication Data
Muir, Frank, 1920–
    A treasury of Christmas.
    I. Muir, Jamie
    394.268282

    ISBN 0 86051 779 9

Printed in Great Britain by St Edmundsbury Press Ltd, Bury St Edmunds, Suffolk

Contents

PREFACE

CHAPTER ONE: **THE BEGINNING OF IT ALL**

A Dickensian Christmas 12

Christmastide 14

A Betjeman Christmas 16

CHAPTER TWO: **31 OCTOBER, ALL-HALLOWS EVE**

The Lord of Misrule 20

The Mummers Play 22

A Mummers Play 25

CHAPTER THREE: **THE SUNDAY BEFORE ADVENT, STIR UP SUNDAY**

Christmas Puddings and Cakes 32

Christmas Cards 33

The Christmas Card Artillery 35

CHAPTER FOUR: **6 DECEMBER, THE FEAST OF ST NICHOLAS**

St Nicholas or Santa Claus 40

Boy Bishops 42

Good King Wenceslas 43

The Shepherd's Calendar 44

CHAPTER FIVE: **21 DECEMBER, ST THOMAS'S DAY**

The Traditions of St Thomas's Day 50

Wassailing 51

Boars' Heads 52

Christmas with the Pooters 54

CHAPTER SIX: **24 DECEMBER, CHRISTMAS EVE**

The Yule Log 58
A Country Parson's Christmas Eve 61
Dumb Cakes 62
Christmas Decorations 62
Mistletoe 63
The Christmas Tree 64
Dickens's Christmas Tree 66
The Kissing Bough 67
The Crib 67
The Old Lad's Passing Bell 68
A Visit from St Nicholas 69

CHAPTER SEVEN: **25 DECEMBER, CHRISTMAS DAY**

Midnight Mass 72
Sowen Cakes and Candles 74
A Cold Christmas Day Morning 75
Christmas Food 76
Mr Pooter Makes a Christmas Speech 77
The Christmas Turkey **78**
Christmas Pudding 79
The Defossilized Plum Pudding 80
Mince Pies 82
Christmas Crackers 83
Christmas Presents 84
Christmas Games 85
The Mistletoe Bough 88
The Bachelor for whom Christmas Coming Once a Year
was more than Enough 90
The Years that Christmas did not Come 91

CHAPTER EIGHT: **26 DECEMBER, BOXING DAY**

Christmas Boxes 94
The Christmas Box Nuisance 95
St Stephen 96
Wren Hunting 97
Grey Mary or Mari Lwyd 99
Hodening 99
Christmas Masques and Pantomimes 99
The Grip of Iron 103

CHAPTER NINE: 27 AND 28 DECEMBER, ST JOHN'S DAY AND HOLY INNOCENTS DAY

The Twelve Days of Christmas	114
St John's Day	114
Holy Innocents Day or Childermas	115
Holy Innocents Day with the Pooters	116

CHAPTER TEN: 31 DECEMBER AND 1 JANUARY, NEW YEAR'S EVE AND NEW YEAR'S DAY

Hogmanay	118
First-Footing	120
A Hogmanay Reminiscence	122
New Year's Day	123

CHAPTER ELEVEN: 5 AND 6 JANUARY, OLD CHRISTMAS EVE AND TWELFTH NIGHT

Old Christmas Eve	128
Fruit Tree Wassailing	129
Journey of the Magi	131
The Twelfth Night Cake	133
The Glastonbury Thorn	135

CHAPTER TWELVE: DISTAFF DAY AND PLOUGH MONDAY

Well, So That is That	138
Distaff Day	140
Plough Monday	140
Index	143

PREFACE

WE ALMOST called this book *A Christmas Pudding* because it is a mixture of many ingredients: the origins of the ancient customs and traditions which we have taken for granted, old pictures, prints and photographs, selections of poetry and prose written about Christmas by authors from W. H. Auden to Charles Dickens, and a complete, previously unpublished melodrama, ready for performance.

It came about because the vicar asked us to consider writing him a Nativity Play, or some other Christmassy piece, which the village could perform, and we found, a bit to our surprise, that we knew almost nothing about Christmas apart from the modern traditions of putting up the tree, decorating a room, exchanging presents, going to church, and eating within an inch of our lives. So we looked into the matter and found to our delight that the origins of Christmas are full of surprises, for instance, St Nicholas, whose name gave us Santa Claus, was a kind of all-purpose Rent-A-Saint who was patron saint of, amongst other august bodies, small boys, Russia, Aberdeen, parish clerks, pawn-brokers, boatmen, dockers, coopers, brewers, travellers, pilgrims, and those who had unjustly lost law suits. And a great many of the customs and traditions which have grown up around the country are inexplicable and hilarious – wren-hunting on the Isle of Man, avoiding 'first-footers' who had flat feet in Northumberland, wassailing the fruit-trees in Somerset by shouting and firing a shotgun at them. We also found that many touching and funny things had been written about Christmas and that there were many old prints and even photographs still available to illustrate the ancient goings-on.

The trouble was that, although there were many books about Christmas to consult, they tended to specialize. One book went thoroughly into the myths, another into the customs, another into pagan origins, etc., but there were few, or perhaps none at that time, which covered the whole field. So we decided to write our own and put down those anecdotes and truths (or half-truths) which we were so delighted to discover. We have arranged the chapters so that the reader is taken steadily through the various larks and celebrations which our ancestors got up to during that wonderful interruption to dreary winter which lies between All Hallows Eve and Plough Monday.

And a Happy New Year.

Frank Muir
Jamie Muir

CHAPTER I

THE BEGINNING
OF IT ALL

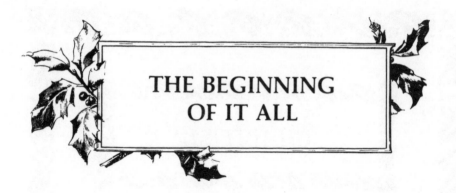

THE BEGINNING
OF IT ALL

A DICKENSIAN CHRISTMAS

CHRISTMAS time! That man must be a misanthrope indeed, in whose breast something like a jovial feeling is not roused – in whose mind some pleasant associations are not awakened – by the recurrence of Christmas. There are people who will tell you that Christmas is not to them what it used to be; that each succeeding Christmas has found some cherished hope, or happy prospect, of the year before, dimmed or passed away; that the present only serves to remind them of reduced circumstances and straitened incomes – of the feasts they once bestowed on hollow friends, and of the cold looks that meet them now, in adversity and misfortune. Never heed such dismal reminiscences. There are few men who have lived long enough in the world, who cannot call up such thoughts any day in the year. Then do not select the merriest of the three hundred and sixty-five for your doleful recollections, but draw your chair nearer the blazing fire – fill the glass and send round the song – and if your room be smaller than it was a dozen years ago, or if your glass be filled with reeking punch, instead of sparkling wine, put a good face on the matter, and empty it off-hand, and fill another, and troll off the old ditty you used to sing, and thank God it's no worse. . .

Who can be insensible to the outpourings of good feeling, and the honest interchange of affectionate attachment which abound at this season of the year. A Christmas family-party! We know nothing in nature more delightful! There seems a magic in the very name of Christmas. Petty jealousies and discords are forgotten; social feelings are awakened, in bosoms to which they have long been strangers; father and son, or brother and sister, who have met and passed with averted gaze, or a look of cold recognition, for months before, proffer and return the cordial embrace, and bury their past animosities in their present happiness. Kindly hearts that have yearned towards each other but have been withheld by false notions of pride and self-dignity, are again reunited, and all is kindness and benevolence! Would that Christmas lasted the whole year through (as it ought) and that the prejudices and passions which deform our better nature were never called into action among those to whom they should ever be strangers!

Charles Dickens-*(Sketches by Boz)* **1836**

Christmastide

Christmas, or a similar festival, has been celebrated from the earliest days of recorded history, and each era and race has pasted a colourful sheet of new customs and traditions over the old.

Telling the story of Christmas is like peeling away centuries of old wallpapers. 'And she brought forth her first-born son and wrapped him up in swaddling clothes and laid him in a manger: because there was no room at the inn.' That was how St Luke described the Nativity; St Matthew provided a few more details: 'Jesus therefore was born in Bethlehem of Judea, in the days of king Herod.'

The early Christians wanted to venerate the birthday of the Saviour but they hit a snag; neither Luke nor Matthew had mentioned the time of day, nor the date in the year. Many and furious debates were held to decide upon a date. During the fourth century the Christians of western Europe settled on 25 December. The Eastern Church at first chose 6 January but by the fifth century they too agreed to 25 December. The reasoning behind this held a happy logic. 25 March was a date sacred since pre-Christian times. The festival of spring, celebrating creation and the return of life to the soil, had always been held on the 25th and the Church took over the date to commemorate the Annunciation of the Virgin, the Church's own celebration of fertility. The date for the Nativity was reached by adding nine months on to 25 March!

25 December was a particularly good date for a Christian festival celebrating new life, because there were several pagan festivals all doing much the same thing. The Romans honoured their god Saturn between 17 and 23 December. Saturnalia was a festival in celebration of Rome's Golden Age, which all hoped one day would return. Many of its festivities became part of the traditional Christmas. On 22 December the Romans held the feast of Brumalia, the birthday of the Unconquered Sun. Brumalia was the equivalent of Christmas to those who worshipped the Persian sun-god Mithras, the most popular of the new religions that had sprung up from the declining Roman Empire, and at one point Christianity's only real pagan rival. When Christianity became the official religion of the Emperor Constantine, in the early part of the fourth century AD, the pagan celebrations on the 25th stayed to become part of Christmas. On 1 January the Romans celebrated *Kalendae Januarii*, a New Year's feast. Connected with this was Juvenalia, the festival of childhood and youth.

Besides these Roman festivals already in existence, there was the Jewish Feast of Lights, Hanuca or Hanukkah, which went on for eight days in late December. This was a celebration of the strength of the Jewish faith, symbolized by the lighting of candles; one the first night, two the next, and so on for eight days. The festival continues to this day; games are played and presents exchanged. The idea of Christ as light of the world was probably adapted by the Church from this Jewish feast.

The date of Christmas also dovetailed in neatly with the winter festival of the Norsemen, Yule, which celebrated the winter solstice and the returning sun. King Hakon the Good actually decreed that the Yule festival should run concurrently with Christmas, and that everyone should brew malt with his ale and keep Yule holy in his own way. Many old pagan customs leaked through into the new Christian festival of Christmas. At first the Church Fathers were appalled by this. Tertullian wrote a *Treatise of Idolatry* in which he proclaimed:

> Let those who have no light in themselves light candles!... Let those over whom Hell fire is hanging fix to their doors laurels doomed presently to burn! You are the light of the world, you are the tree ever green. If you have renounced temples, make not your own house a temple.

But this was not the way to cope with the old pagan customs. In 597 St Augustine and a small group of missionaries landed in Kent to preach Christianity to the Anglo-Saxons. St Gregory, the Pope who had sent them on this mission, offered advice on the problem of the pagan customs and superstitions. The Venerable Bede took down his words:

> The idol temples of that race should by no means be destroyed, but only the idols in them. Take holy water and sprinkle it in these shrines, build altars and place relics in them. For if the shrines are well built, it is essential they should be changed from the worship of the devils to the service of the true God. When this people see that their shrines are not destroyed they will be able to banish error from their hearts and be more ready to come to the places they are familiar with, but now recognising and worshipping the true God.

The Church applied the same principle to the pagan festivals. They were not condemned, instead they were given an alternative Christian significance. St Gregory's advice won the day for Christianity in Britain, but Christmas never completely shed its pagan associations.

A BETJEMAN CHRISTMAS

The bells of waiting Advent ring,
The Tortoise stove is lit again
And lamp-oil light across the night
Has caught the streaks of winter rain
In many a stained-glass window sheen
From Crimson Lake to Hooker's Green.

The holly in the windy hedge
And round the Manor House the yew
Will soon be stripped to deck the ledge,
The altar, font and arch and pew,
So that the villagers can say
'The church looks nice' on Christmas Day.

Provincial public houses blaze
And Corporation tramcars clang,
On lighted tenements I gaze
Where paper decorations hang,
And bunting in the red Town Hall
Says 'Merry Christmas to you all.'

And London shops on Christmas Eve
Are strung with silver bells and flowers
As hurrying clerks the city leave
To pigeon-haunted classic towers,
And marbled clouds go scudding by
The many-steepled London sky.

And girls in slacks remember Dad,
And oafish louts remember Mum,
And sleepless children's hearts are glad,
And Christmas-morning bells say 'Come!'
Even to the shining ones who dwell
Safe in the Dorchester Hotel.

Mummers in their traditional costume, from a photograph taken at
Minstead, Hampshire by Sir Benjamin Stone in 1912

The transformation of St Nicholas into the familiar figure of Santa Claus:
Left illustration from Clement Moore's *Visit of St Nicholas,* 1848; *Right*
Thomas Nast's prototype of today's Father Christmas, engraved for
Harper's Weekly, c. 1870

Two contenders for the title of the first Christmas card: *above* John Horsley's card of 1846; *below* William Maw Egley's card, with the much-discussed last digit in the date — 1842 or 1848?

And is it true? And is it true,
This most tremendous tale of all,
Seen in a stained-glass window's hue,
A Baby in an ox's stall?
The Maker of the stars and sea
Become a Child on earth for me?

And is it true? For if it is,
No loving fingers tying strings
Around those tissued fripperies,
The sweet and silly Christmas things,
Bath salts and inexpensive scent
And hideous tie so kindly meant,

No love that in a family dwells,
No carolling in frosty air,
Nor all the steeple-shaking bells
Can with this single Truth compare –
That God was Man in Palestine
And lives today in Bread and Wine.

Sir John Betjeman *(A Few Late Chrysanthemums)* **1954**

CHAPTER II

31 OCTOBER,

ALL-HALLOWS EVE

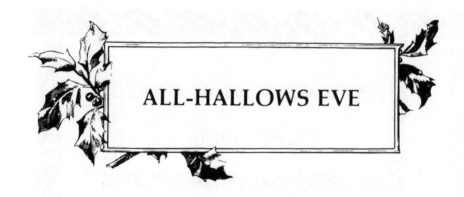

The Lord of Misrule

ALL-HALLOWS EVE, 31 October, was traditionally the day on which the Lord of Misrule was appointed for the Christmas to come. He would then reign through till Candlemas, 2 February. Known by other names, 'The Master of Merry Disport', 'The Abbot of Unreason', 'Christmas King', it was his appointed task to ensure continuous merriment from New Year's Eve through to Twelfth Night. The Lord of Misrule was the personification of the spirit of disorder, fun and merrymaking which made the Christmas holidays something to look forward to in the Middle Ages, a welcome break during the hard winter months.

Like most Christmas traditions, the reign of the Lord of Misrule and his mock court combined certain characteristics from two earlier festivities. The Feast of Fools, once celebrated by the lower clergy on 1 January – the Feast of the Circumcision – was similarly an occasion for riotous and disorderly revels. Ecclesiastical ritual was parodied, the higher officials of the Church swapped places with the lower, and everyone larked about wearing masks. In its election of a mock bishop or pope and the wearing of masks, the Feast of Fools had in fact poached elements from the Roman celebrations at Saturnalia. The Romans used to elect a mock king and give their slaves the freedom to say and do whatever they liked. Grotesque masks were worn and men dressed up as women and vice versa.

Records exist of a Lord of Misrule at the court of Edward III when he spent Christmas at Guildford in 1348. Orders were issued for a 'large number of masks – some with the faces of women, some with beards, some like angel heads of silver'. Leading noblemen had a Lord of Misrule elected from the lower orders in their house at Christmas, as did Sheriffs, Lord Mayors, Oxford colleges and Inns of Court. The Church, rigidly hierarchical, took rather a dim view of some of the goings-on. Church reformers protested against the title of 'Abbot of

Unreason' in the twelfth, thirteenth, fourteenth and fifteenth centuries; and no doubt sighed with relief when it finally died out in the sixteenth. In the Elizabethan era the Lords of Misrule used to lead their 'courts' into the church to disrupt the service, as they had done during the Feast of Fools. This practice was heavily criticized by the Puritan, Philip Stubbes, in his *Anatomie of Abuses* (1583):

> *The wildheads of the parish, conventing together, choose them a Grand-Captain (of all mischief) whom they ennoble with the title of my Lord of Misrule, and him they crown with great solemnity and adopt their king. This king anointed, chooseth forth twenty, forty, threescore or a hundred lusty guts, like to himself, to wait upon his lordly majesty, and to guard his noble person... Then march this heathen company towards the church and churchyard, their pipers piping, their drummers thundering, their stumps dancing, their bells jingling, their handkerchiefs swinging abut their heads like madmen, their hobbyhorses and other monsters skirmishing amongst the throng; and in this sort they go to church (I say) and into the church (though the Minister be at prayer or preaching), dancing and swinging their handkerchiefs... like devils incarnate with such a confused noise, that no man can hear his own voice. Then the foolish people they look, they stare, they laugh, they fleer, and mount upon forms and pews to see these goodly pageants solemnised in this sort.*

The Lords of Misrule gave themselves elaborate titles parodying their masters. One in the reign of Queen Elizabeth called himself 'The high and mighty Prince Henry, Prince of Purpoole, Archduke of Stapulia and Bernadin, Duke of High and Nether Holborn, Marquis of St Giles and Tottenham, Count Palatine of Bloomsbury and Clerkenwell, Great Lord of the Cantons of Islington, Kentish Town, Paddington and Knightsbridge, Knight of the Most Heroical Order of the Helmet and Sovereign of the same'. At the Inner Temple another Lord of Misrule gave the following names to his 'courtiers': 'Sir Francis Flatterer of Fowlehurst in the county of Buckingham, Sir Randle Rakabite of Rascall-Hall in the county of Rakehell, Sir Morgan Mumchance of Much Monkery in the county of Mad Mopery, Sir Batholomew Baldbreech of Buttocksbury in the county of Breckneck.'

The Lord of Misrule was a principal ingredient in the medieval celebration of Christmas. However, his revelries were far too pagan for the Puritans of the seventeenth century who violently attacked him and eventually banned his election altogether. When Charles II succeeded to the throne the elections could have started up again, but they didn't. Perhaps the Lord of Misrule had been forgotten, or perhaps the court had become more sophisticated, but no one bothered to elect him any more. It is nice to think that the spirit of the old pagan Lords of Misrule has not quite died out. In the armed forces it is still customary for the officers to serve their men Christmas dinner.

The Mummers Play

The word 'Mummer' could have derived from either the German *mumme*, which meant 'a mask' or 'masker', or the Greek *momme* which meant 'a child's bugbear', 'an ogress', or 'a frightening mask'. The word could also have emerged from the way in which the Mummers spoke their lines through masks; the sound that came out was a mumble.

All-Hallows Eve was the beginning of the season for performing Mummers plays. Traditionally, all the performances took place between All-Hallows Eve and Easter. In the Middle Ages these were thought of as the months of winter. It is still possible to see a Mummers play today, though now they tend to be rather folksy celebrations of Merrie England and almost completely devoid of any meaning or purpose. Much shouting and clashing of wooden swords, references to Bold Slasher and the Turkish Knight, people feigning death only to be revived with some elixir – the medieval equivalent of Popeye's spinach – and then it is all over and the collecting tins are out.

Yet Mummers were once to be found in nearly every village in England. Together with the mystery and miracle plays, they were the survivals of pre-Reformation folk drama. But unlike the mystery and miracle plays, they were distinctly non-Christian in character. Their symbolism was pagan. In the Mummers plays a character was killed as the crops of the earth are killed by the frozen months of winter. Soon spring would come again, and the dramatic representation of the rebirth of the crops was the revival of the slain man by the doctor character. Each year the Mummers would meet at All-Hallows Eve or thereabouts and rehearse their traditional lines, words handed down from generation to generation. Often sons would follow their fathers into the same rôle, but be told only their part and the cue lines from the speech before. This somewhat fallible method of passing on the Mummers play in the oral tradition may largely account for its near-incomprehensible dialogue.

The cast usually consisted of six to eight men, never women; the women were expected to make the 'disguises'. These were fairly elaborate assemblages because the essential purpose of the costume was to hide the wearer's identity; hence they were called 'disguises' and not costumes. To be recognized broke the 'luck' the performers brought. Mummers' disguises were usually masks or blackened faces and fringes of cloth sewn on to clothes turned inside out. They must have provided a considerable degree of anonymity, because criminals used these disguises to such an extent that in the third year of Henry VIII's reign, an act was passed to stop this happening. People were forbidden to keep 'vizors' for mumming inside their houses. Flouting this law could cost twenty shillings and wearing the mask meant three months' imprisonment.

The characters were led in by Father Christmas. A typical example of his opening speech went:

Here comes I, Father Christmas am I,
Welcome – or welcome not;
I hope olde Father Christmas
Will never be forgot...
... Christmas comes but once a year,
When it comes it brings good cheer;
With a pocket full of money
And a cellar full of beer,
Roast beef, plum pudding and mince pie,
Who likes them better than I?

Although nothing is certain about these plays, which exist in many versions, they probably found their form at the time of the Crusades. Thus the hero was generally called Saint or King George, and his opponent the Turkish Knight. Other characters were named Bold Slasher, the Quack Doctor, Valiant Soldier, Lawyer, Twing Twang, Little Johnnie Jack, Rumour, Hector, Alexander and, later, Nelson. The villain was often given the name of a real person: Oliver Cromwell; Napoleon; Tippoo or Admiral Byng. The name Napoleon was particularly popular along the south coast of England during the invasion threat at the beginning of the nineteenth century.

The curious plot generally unfolded as follows. After the club-wielding Father Christmas had set the scene, the Turkish Knight confronted Saint or King George. (The succession of the three Hanoverian Georges in the eighteenth century, one after another, seems to have established the hero of the Mummers play as King rather than St George). The knight would cry:

In comes I the Turkey Snipe,
Come from my Turkish Land to fight.

George then challenged him to a fight and killed him. But he suffered pangs of remorse:

Only behold and see what I have been and done,
Cut and slain my brother just like the evening sun.

The Doctor was summoned and promptly appeared. He was a much-travelled man. 'I've travelled India, South India and Bendigo.' In some versions he would claim to have visited the surreal town of 'Itty-Titty, where there's neither wall nor city'. He had just the right medicine to revive fallen knights:

> *I carry a little bottle by my side*
> *Which is called the Opliss Poppliss Drops.*

Or in another version:

> *I'll cure him for a pound:*
> *I have a little bottle of Elucumpane.*

The Doctor administered his potion:

> *Here Jack, take a little of this flip-flop,*
> *Pour it down thy tip-top.*

The Turk revived and all trooped off, often singing a carol and rattling their collecting box, which probably became the main reason for performing the Mummers play.

Nevertheless, the magic of the rebirth of spring and the impersonation of the slain god at the Winter Solstice was still there. It must have been fairly impossible to grasp, though, especially as the form of the play and the details within it kept taking on different shapes down the years as local colour and topical references were absorbed. A villain in one of the Yorkshire versions introduced himself:

> *In come I a suffragette. Over my shoulder I carry my clogs.*

Perhaps the most popular evening for a performance of a Mummers play was Christmas Eve. Thomas Hardy, in *The Return of the Native*, describes one such visit. The Mummers would group outside the door of the Big House and wait till they thought the moment right. Then they would hammer on the door, Father Christmas would enter and begin the play with his stentorian bellow. All of which is a long way from the self-conscious, though worthy, efforts of the revivalists.

A MUMMERS PLAY

This is the full text of a traditional Mummers play. It was performed annually at Chadlington, a small town in Oxfordshire, and the words were taken down in 1893:

FATHER CHRISTMAS [*reciting whilst walking around*]:
Here comes I old Father Christmas.
Christmas comes but once a year,
When it comes it brings good cheer.
Roast beef and plum pudding
And plenty of good old English beer.
Last Christmas time I turned the spit
I burnt my finger and I can't find of it;
Then a spark fled over the table,
Saucepan got up and beat the ladle.
Said the gridiron, 'Can't you two agree?
I am the justice, bring them in to me.'
I brought the broom to sweep the room.
I brought a brush, so pick him up
And all my jolly company.
Good master and mistress, I hope you are all within,
For I come this merry Christmas time to see you and your kin.
I hope you won't be fronted, nor still take any offence,
For if you do, pray tell to me
And I'll be gone before I commence.
Oh, room for a gallant soldier!
Oh, room to give him rise.
I'll show you the very best activity
That's shown on the common stage.
If you don't believe me what I say,
Step in, King George and clear the way.

[*Enter KING GEORGE*]

KING GEORGE:
I'm King George, this notable knight,
I shed my blood for England's right.
England's right and England's glory all maintain.

[*Enter BULLSLASHER*]

BULLSLASHER:
I am the gallant soldier,
Bullslasher is my name;
Sword and buckle by my side,
I mean to win the game.
First I draw my sword,
Then thy precious blood.

KING GEORGE:
Don't thou be so hot, Bullslasher!
Don't thou see in the room another man
Thou has got to fight.

BULLSLASHER:
A battle, a battle betwixt thee and me
To see which on the ground dead first shall be.
Mind the lists and guard the blows
Mind thy head and thy poor old soul.

[KING GEORGE and BULLSLASHER fight. KING GEORGE falls to the ground.]

FATHER CHRISTMAS:
Come in, Jack Finney.

[Enter JACK FINNEY]

JACK FINNEY:
My name is not Jack but Master Finney.
Do you know I am a man of great Faith!
Do as much as or any other man.

FATHER CHRISTMAS:
Then cure this man.

JACK FINNEY:
The case is now as it was before.
Rise up King George and fight once more.

[KING GEORGE gets up and the fight recommences. He is again killed by BULLSLASHER.]

FATHER CHRISTMAS:
Oh Doctor! Doctor, haste away!
Don't thou longer make delay
For our best man is wounded
Through the heart and through the knee.
Ten thousand pounds I fear will not cure he!

JACK FINNEY:
What will you give for a good doctor? Ten pounds?

FATHER CHRISTMAS:
No such money!

JACK FINNEY:
Five pounds then?

FATHER CHRISTMAS:
No such money, but five farthings will I give, but no more.

JACK FINNEY:
Then let the Doctor in.

[Enter DOCTOR]

DOCTOR:
Here come I the notable Doctor.
I have brought some pills to cure all ills
And others to come.

FATHER CHRISTMAS:
Whence dost thou come from, my notable Doctor?

DOCTOR:
Oh! all diseases!
Just what my box pleases.
Hard corns, soft corns,
Hipips, the phipps and palsy,
The gout and pains within
And pains all around about.

FATHER CHRISTMAS:
Then cure this man!

DOCTOR:
What is the matter, my old man?
[To JACK FINNEY]:
Give him a pill, Jack.

JACK FINNEY:
Give him one thyself!

DOCTOR:
What's that you say?

JACK FINNEY:
Just a–going to, aren't I?

[*They wrangle in this way. At last they belabour the fallen KING GEORGE with a bladder at the end of a stick.*]

DOCTOR [*To King George*]:
Do you feel any better?

[*KING GEORGE mumbles something.*]

JACK FINNEY:
What does he say, Doctor?

DOCTOR:
That he has the toothache.

JACK FINNEY:
Then let us have it out.

DOCTOR:
Where are my pliers?

JACK FINNEY:
Fetch 'em thyself.

DOCTOR:
What's that?

JACK FINNEY:
Just a-going to, aren't I?

DOCTOR:
Now thee have broke 'em. What didst do that for?

JACK FINNEY:
Couldn't help it. Fell over that long, narrow, crooked stile. Broke 'em a-purpose.

DOCTOR:
What's that?

JACK FINNEY:
Couldn't help it.

[*They again wrangle in this way. The DOCTOR places himself over the fallen KING GEORGE. The others take one another round the waist to enable the DOCTOR to extract the tooth, which after some time is done, all falling over as a result.*]

DOCTOR:
Look at this elephant's tooth!
See what quick quack doctors can do!

[*Then the DOCTOR and JACK FINNEY try to raise the fallen KING at last assisting him to rise with the aid of the bladder.*]

Come in, Helseybub.

[*Enter HELSEYBUB*]

HELSEYBUB:
In comes I old Helseybub
On my back I carries a tub,
In my hand a dripping pan –
Don't you think I am a jolly old man?

[*All walk round and retire*]

CHAPTER III

THE SUNDAY
BEFORE ADVENT,

STIR UP SUNDAY

STIR UP SUNDAY

Christmas Puddings and Cakes

STIR UP Sunday is the popular and splendid name for the Sunday before Advent. By tradition it was the last occasion on which Christmas puddings and cakes could be begun if they were to be ready by 25 December. Surprisingly, the name has nothing to do with stirring the pudding mixture. It was called Stir Up Sunday after the Collect in the service for that day: 'Stir up we beseech thee, O Lord, the wills of thy faithful people, that they plenteously bringing forth the fruit of good works; may of thee be plenteously rewarded.' As the Sundays of the Church year are governed by the movability of Easter, Stir Up Sunday does not fall on the same day each year; nevertheless it always falls within the last half of November.

Plum porridge was the earliest form of plum pudding, and like mince pies, it was originally not sweet at all but made with meat. An early recipe states that beef and veal should be boiled together with sack – a once popular wine from the Canary Isles – old hock, sherry, lemon and orange juice. To this was added sugar, raisins, currants, prunes – the dried plums which gave their name to the mixture – cochineal, cinnamon and cloves. The whole thing was thickened with brown bread. The even stiffer eighteenth-century version of this was the ancestor of our Christmas pudding, and meat was left out early in the nineteenth century.

The notion of putting silver trinkets and charms into the pudding probably came from the earlier traditions of the beans inside the Twelfth Night cake, but this has since died out. It is still traditional to bury a silver coin in the mixture. To begin with it was a silver farthing, then a penny. After the Great War it was the smallest silver coin, a threepenny bit, or Joey. When that went out of circulation it was a sixpence. To fulfil tradition now, one should insert 5p. Another example of inflation! All the family should stir the pudding mixture in

St Nicholas slips a purse through the poor man's window as
dowry for his daughters. Late fifteenth-century painting by
Gerard David

WISH-
ING
YOU A
TOO TOO
MERRY
CHRIST
MAS

An 'aesthetic' Father Christmas: a reflection of the vogue of the
1880s

turn and make a wish at the same time. The coin should then be shoved in, plus a ring and a thimble; the coin is to bring worldly fortune, the ring a marriage and the thimble a life of blessedness.

Christmas cake is a much later tradition, only appearing in the middle of the nineteenth century. It was really only plum pudding further solidified, without the alcohol, so as to make it suitable for family tea, which as a meal dates back no further than Victoria's reign. From the 1870s onwards the decoration of the Christmas cake was treated with high seriousness and specially-made decorations were sold. From Germany came architectural monstrosities depicting, in china, Father Christmas coming down a chimney. After the Great War the Christmas catalogues of large department stores offered models of Father Christmas riding a motor-bike, riding an elephant, and scrambling out of an igloo.

Christmas Cards

There is considerable debate as to who devised the first Christmas card. The most reasonable claim is probably Henry Cole, who became Sir Henry, the first director of the newly-founded Victoria and Albert Museum. In November 1843 he wrote in his diary: 'Mr Horsley came and brought design for Christmas card.' A thousand lithographed copies of John Horsley's design were made in 1846. It showed a family brimming with good cheer, surrounded by rustic trellis-work. Two smaller frames on either side depicted Christmassy charitable acts: 'Clothing the Naked' and 'Feeding the Hungry'. The card was hand-coloured and put on sale through Felix Summerly's Treasure House, a shop which Cole had helped to set up in Bond Street.

Another contender for the First Christmas Card was W. C. T. Dobson, R.A. In 1844 he sent a friend a sketch he had made which symbolized for him the spirit of Christmas. The next year he had copies lithographed, which he sent to all his friends. Though this card was a year earlier than Cole's, not many people knew of its existence because it was never actually for sale. A third contender for the title was William Maw Egley. His claim is complicated by a badly written number which may be either an 8 or a 3. If it is a 3, then Egley was the first, but he would have been only sixteen at the time. His card was like Horsley's; three arcaded panels and a vision of Charitable Acts. Finally there is the claim of a vicar from Newcastle, the Reverend Edward Bradley, who wrote best-sellers under the pseudonym of Cuthbert Bede. He had a card made for circulation amongst his friends.

Horsley and Cole would seem to be favourites because they put a Christmas card up for sale. It took a further ten years for the idea to catch on. The *Illustrated London News* first advertised Christmas stationery in December 1863. *Punch* first made mention of Christmas cards in 1868, and *The Times* in 1871. Printing expenses held Christmas cards back at first but the invention of the chromolithographic process led to cheap colour reproduction, which brought the price of cards within the reach of most people.

The cards of the early 1870s were often more like Valentines than Christmas cards. This was probably because they were usually put out by firms who already sold Valentine's Day cards. Christmas cards and Valentines often shared the same picture, with a different sentiment beneath. The pictures went in for heavily laced borders, garlands of flowers, cherubs and young men in eighteenth-century costume. These soon gave way to strong Christmassy themes. Examples of the work of the book illustrator, C. H. Bennett, show Christmas bells, Christmas fare and cupids shovelling Christmas puddings into wheelbarrows. Others depict traditional scenes: the village church, its roof groaning under snow several feet thick, and plenty of children, snowballing, ice-skating and hauling in the Yule log.

Nevertheless, it was the robin that came to epitomize the Christmas card Christmas. Warmly greeted during the winter months for its boldness and friendliness to humans – admirable virtues wholly in keeping with the sentiments of Christmas – card designers and manufacturers turned a blind eye to the fact that the robin is notoriously beastly to other birds. But long before the Victorians and their cards, the robin with its red breast was held in special esteem at Christmas time as a symbol of fire and new life in an otherwise barren landscape. Postmen in Victoria's reign were called 'robin postmen' because of their red uniforms. Blue-clad policemen were less fortunate – they were dubbed 'bluebottles'.

Christmas cards are the product less of the traditional Christmas than its romantic revival, of which the most celebrated champion was Charles Dickens with *A Christmas Carol* and his description of Mr Pickwick's Christmas at Dingly Dell. The vision of Christmas celebrations as described by Dickens in his Christmas books was so hypnotic that he virtually invented the Victorian Christmas. Other people had less romantic ideas. The Lord Mayor of Birmingham's Christmas card for 1909 depicted Santa flying low over the city dispensing the largesse of a municipal corporation: trams, electric lights, dust-carts, baths and policemen. The Church similarly hit upon the Christmas card as a missionary device. The Society for Promoting Christian Knowledge began to encourage religious themes on cards, printing their own as a guiding light.

The traditional Christmas rush first started with the introduction of a special halfpenny card stamp in 1870. In 1880 the Postmaster-General issued the first of many pleas: 'Post Early for Christmas'. At that time he also pleaded: 'Post Early for Valentine's Day'. But the Christmas card was not without some Scrooge-like opposition. A correspondent wrote to *The Times* after the Christmas rush of 1877, saying that the sending of such cards was 'a social evil' and complaining bitterly at 'the delay of legitimate correspondence by cartloads of children's cards'.

THE CHRISTMAS CARD ARTILLERY

During the next three days about 350,000,000 Christmas cards will be fired in the British Isles.

Most of them are aimed at targets at home, for the long-ranged salvoes for overseas have been loosed off and are nearing their point of impact. Now I am an old gunner in the Christmas Card Artillery, and it seems to me that more should be known of the military postal science of causing Yuletide mortification, annoyance, irritation, inconvenience, vexation, offence, resentment and deep anger.

The whole practice is such a thundering nuisance that it is high time that some practical advantage such as causing unhappiness was extracted out of the wretched business. I think I can point the way. The first – and one of the most essential things to decide – is when to shoot. Timing is of critical importance. A premature Christmas card is not only ineffective but can be downright humiliating to the sender. It reveals one's position, discloses the size and weight of the ammunition and often provokes a devastating counter-attack.

On the other hand a late Christmas card (we gunners call them 'hangfires') is liable to explode harmlessly, for the enemy has been given time to take cover. It is better to be on the early rather than late side, for the get-in-quick Christmas card sets the pace and compels the opposition to reply. The next thing to understand is the value of size in Christmas cards. Important people – and people who think they are important – send big and important-looking Christmas cards. This makes the recipient feel small – which is precisely what was intended. Expensive Christmas cards can be deadly, too, for they are usually fired by expensive people to make their victims feel cheap. This is often quite costly but well worth it.

The really big Christmas card can be immensely infuriating. It barges its way into your house, glows with the swank and pride of its sender, crowds everything off the mantelpiece and makes strangers cry 'Ooooh' as they pick it up to see who is so rich, so powerful and so magnificent, as to be able to afford it. The very small Christmas card can be pretty insulting, too. Don't underestimate its destructive value. It shows what you think of the addressee – practically nothing. It is a mistake to make them too small as they then become rather cute and are liable to give pleasure. Avoid this dangerous mistake. A really contemptuous size is about three and a half inches by two and a half inches. They are a bit difficult to obtain in the shops just now but are well worth the suffering they cause.

An old gunner's trick can be used very effectively, if, when you've sent a really whopping great card, you get an even bigger one in return. You fire a second round. You wait till after Christmas and then you send off the most squalid printed missile you can find. Address it incorrectly – but not so inaccurately as to confuse the postman – and then carefully spell the target's name wrong. By this crafty means you create an unbearable impression that the first card was all a mistake and that the grubby follow-up is the true appraisal of your contemptuous feelings. Much misery and deep and very valuable loathing can be created by this well-proven and disgusting practice.

Now from size and cost to content. With a little thought, the malevolent Christmas-carder can gain the upper hand of whole nations at a time. Do you know any of those characters who live in Scotland? Then no doubt you burn to have your revenge. It is quite easy. Buy a Christmas card with a Scotsman on the front of it. Automatically he will be red-nosed (whusky), horns-woggled and be-sticked (Harry Lauder) and kilted (fra the Hie'lan's). The red nose will offend, the stick will be criticised for its music-hall background and, as for the tartan, nothing can stop its being one hundred percent wrong. Nobody, least of all designers and printers, gets the patterns right. But these are minor (although valuable) irritations. The real razor slash is in the inscription. Now, the way to tear Scotland apart and wrap it up in a torn Christmas card, is to smash into the Rabbie Burns business. What goes under the doddering alcoholic crackpot from Auchtermuchtie, runs something like this:

Ah the whaupit, gurnin' dochter
Frae the brawlie speering dichter
Sonsy gaes the loupin' beastie
Whaur's the crowlin' ferlie cochter.

Now that's pretty good Burns. The real Midlothian
buttermilk touch. The Scots-wha-hae-wi'-Wallace-bled mob
see this patriotic stuff and immediately start arguing as
to whether the poem came from *Man was Made to Mourn* or
The Lass of Ballochmyle by the immortal R.B. They quarrel.
They fight. They fall out. 'It wasn't frae *The Lass of Ballochmyle*,
nor from *The Kirk of Lamington.*' In their Hie'lan' disagreements
they even hit each other. This is deeply gratifying south
of the Border, because anybody can write Burns. I can
write Burns. And that delectable sonnet on the card is my
particular piece of Burns.

Another intensely valuable and hurtful approach is the
Out-of-Season Touch. This studiously and carefully avoids
robins, holly, snow, log-fires and wassail. People stuffed
with Christmas pudding, South African port and crystallized
ginger can be turned dizzy, green and reeling with the
vertigoes by one glimpse of the front of a Christmas card
of the Cutty Sark in full sail. This number, which even in
mid-summer is enough to give you the dry heaves, is available
almost everywhere at a reasonable price. Strongly
recommended and of great emetic value.

Anti-dog lovers (Britain, contrary to popular conception,
is laden down to the gunnels with 'em) can be estranged
for evermore with Christmas cards of lop-eared spaniels
and unbearable pekes with hideously insulting tails like
furry aspidistras. Likewise, anti-catmen and anti-catgirls
can be sent howling and spitting over the tiles by presenting
them with carefully selected pictures of Tiddles, Cuddles
and Snookey – the yelling, sharp-clawed, slit-eyed
limbs of Satan.

William Connor: Cassandra of the *Daily Mirror,* **21 December 1953**

CHAPTER IV

6 DECEMBER,

THE FEAST OF ST NICHOLAS

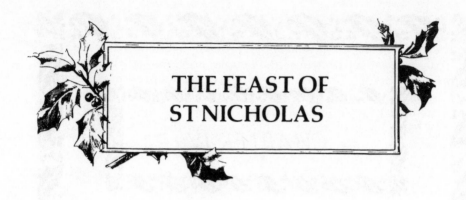

THE FEAST OF ST NICHOLAS

St Nicholas or Santa Claus

ST NICHOLAS really is the most extraordinary saint. Very little is known about him except that he was born in Lycia, one of the many small provinces of the Roman Empire in Asia Minor, lived there all his life, became its Archbishop, and died there sometime in the early part of the fourth century AD. Many stories sprouted up about him and he rapidly became one of the most popular saints of the Middle Ages. In fact, he was so popular that he was adopted as patron saint by, among others, Russia, Aberdeen, parish clerks, pawnbrokers, boatmen, fishermen, dockers, coopers, brewers, travellers, pilgrims and those who had unjustly lost lawsuits. However, he is principally remembered as the patron saint of boys. The story of St Nicholas and the three boys in the brine tub is probably the origin of this special rôle.

According to this legend, while St Nicholas was on his way to the Council of Nicea – where he is remembered for punching the ear of an unorthodox patriarch named Arius – he stopped off at an inn. The owner had just murdered three small boys and, like his Victorian counterpart Sweeney Todd, had cut up the bodies and salted them down to be sold as meat for pies. St Nicholas, realizing what had happened, made the sign of the cross over the tub and the three boys emerged singing praises to God. He then promptly converted the innkeeper to stop the same thing happening again.

As the patron saint of boys and girls, St Nicholas's feast day was remembered by giving children small presents of gilt gingerbread or toys. On the Continent it was traditional for somebody to dress up and pretend to be St Nicholas. On the eve of 6 December the children were instructed to leave out hay, straw and carrots for his horse; in the morning they would find that he, in return, had left them a present each. It was because he was such a useful, all-purpose saint that the Church gave him this important Christmas job as well as looking after children, Russia, Aberdeen, pawnbrokers and the rest.

Since pagan times it had been traditional to give presents at mid-winter. The Romans gave presents during their Saturnalia festival, and the men of the North worshipped the god Woden, who rode across the frozen wastes to bring his people presents in the depths of winter. Long before Christianity, people expected presents. Obviously the Church could not let people carry on believing that Woden would bring them, so St Nicholas was brought in to solve the problem in order that the pagan custom might continue under the thoroughly respectable patronage of a saint, whose name was now simplified to 'Santa Claus'. This is the reason why each 6 December, parents tell their children to write notes to St Nicholas, i.e. Santa Claus, asking for the toys they would like for Christmas. Traditionally these notes should be left on a window sill, or just inside the chimney, not so that Daddy can find out what offensive plastic weapon his child wants for Xmas, but so that St Nicholas can reach them easily. This part of the tradition may originate in the legend of the poor man about to prostitute his daughters, for whom St Nicholas left three round bags full of gold on the window ledge. Another version of the same story says that St Nicholas threw the bag of gold into the house through an open window and it fell into a stocking hung up to dry. Hence, perhaps, the Christmas stocking.

In Bavaria, St Nicholas was thought of only as a message-runner. He took the children's requests up to heaven but it was a representative of the Infant Jesus who actually brought them to the houses on Christmas morning. They called him *Liebes Christkind* (Dear Christ Child), which in America became corrupted to 'Kriss Kringle'. But in England, where the pagan elements that make up the traditions of Christmas are less hidden, it is Santa Claus who comes back with the Christmas presents.

After the Protestant Reformation in Europe there was considerably less emphasis on the worship of saints, and this included St Nicholas. To reduce his popish, saint-like qualities he was gradually merged with the red-faced, pagan, holly-crowned, club-swinging Father Christmas, who was already familiar from the Mummers plays. In an attempt to purge the Christmas present-bringer of his corrupt associations, the Protestant reformers had inadvertently given a pagan idol a new lease of life.

This Father Christmas was a rakish fellow; red robe wide open at the chest, face flushed – almost certainly from wine – a crown of phallic holly on his head; his image was not entirely U-certificate. It was the Americans who took him in and smartened him up. The picture of Santa in the mind's eye, the loveable old man with white hair and whiskers, red coat and cap (in Britain he wore a hood) riding along on his sleigh, all these are American inventions of the nineteenth century. The first of Santa's tailors was Thomas Nast who, in *Harper's Illustrated Weekly* of 1863 and for successive years, drew versions of the poet Clement Clarke Moore's St Nick and called him Santa Claus. To begin with, his Santa wore a jump-suit of fur and a little round hat, but he did have the beard and whiskers, sleigh and reindeer.

Perhaps the men who were first employed by large department stores to impersonate him helped introduce the mock-medieval red gown instead of the furry jump-suit. To 'ho-ho-ho' in Santa's Cavern while handing out presents to howling children must have been bad enough without the indignity of wearing a romper suit. It may be a sign of the times that it was felt necessary in New York, in 1914, to found a Santa Claus Association 'to preserve children's faith in Santa Claus'. This association answered all mail marked 'To Santa Claus', which was handed in to them by the Post Office.

Boy Bishops

Another rather peculiar medieval St Nicholas's Day custom was the election of Boy Bishops. On this day, in many schools up and down the country, the pupils would elect one of their friends to be the Boy Bishop. Amongst the first references to this was that Edward I's gift of forty shillings to the performers after hearing the Boy Bishop's service at Heton near Newcastle-on-Tyne in 1299. The seventeenth-century historian, John Strype, described the tradition:

> This Boy Bishop, or St Nicholas, was commonly one of the choristers, and therefore in the old offices episcopus choristarum, bishop of the choristers, and chosen by the rest for this honour. But afterward there were many St Nicholases, and every parish almost had its St Nicholas. And from St Nicholas' Day to Innocents' Day at night, this boy bore the name of a bishop, and the state and habit too, wearing the mitre and the pastoral staff, and the rest of the pontifical attire; nay, and reading the holy offices. While he went his procession, he was much feasted and treated by the people, as it seems much valuing his blessing, which made the citizens so fond of keeping this holiday.

The Boy Bishop was also permitted to elect his friends as canons and priests. If he died during the time he was a bishop he was buried with the honours of a real bishop. There is the tomb of one in Salisbury Cathedral.

Presumably the idea of the Boy Bishop, besides celebrating St Nicholas's feast, was to interest the children in the Church as a possible career; just as the papers used to print a photograph of a small boy dressed in an army uniform alongside a squadron of infantrymen, with an interview beneath in which the child always said that he wanted to be a soldier when he grew up. Perhaps the Boy Bishop ceremony shared some of the elements of army recruiting.

The Boy Bishop tradition was offensive to the Protestant reformers of Henry VIII's reign and the ceremony was suppressed in 1542. It was revived by the Catholic Queen Mary, though rather as a Christmas jollity than as anything else, and it finally sank for good in the reign of Elizabeth I.

Good King Wenceslas

Good King Wenceslas is a rather mysterious figure in the traditions of Christmas. He was a Bohemian nobleman of the tenth century, who lived till he was twenty-six and was then murdered by his mother, Drahomira, and his brother, Boleslav. His story, short as it is, probably first reached English ears when James I's daughter Elizabeth married the Elector Palatine, the ruler of Bohemia. He seems hardly worth a mention, except that his is the only Christmas carol we can play on the mouth-organ.

THE SHEPHERD'S CALENDAR

John Clare, who lived during the early years of the nineteenth century, was a poor farm labourer who turned poet. His first volume of poems was entitled 'Poems, descriptive of Rural Life and Scenery, by John Clare, a Northamptonshire peasant', which gives a good clue as to the sort of poetry he wrote and the sort of background he came from. The following extract, from The Shepherd's Calendar, *describes what Christmas was like in the 1820s for a poor farming community.*

Christmass is come and every hearth
Makes room to give him welcome now
E'en want will dry its tears in mirth
And crown him wi' a holly bough
Tho' tramping 'neath a winter's sky
O'er snowy track paths and ryhmey stiles
The huswife sets her spining bye
And bids him welcome wi' her smiles

Each house is swept the day before
And windows stuck wi' evergreens
The snow is beesom'd from the door
And comfort crowns the cottage scenes
Gilt holly wi' its thorny pricks
And yew and box wi' berrys small
These deck the unus'd candlesticks
And pictures hanging by the wall

Neighbours resume their anual cheer
Wishing wi' smiles and spirits high
Glad Christmass and a happy year
To every morning passer-by
Milk maids their Christmass journeys go
Accompanyd wi't favour'd swain
And childern pace the crumping snow
To taste their granny's cake again

Hung wi' the ivys veining bough
The ash trees round the cottage farm
Are often stript of branches now
The cotter's Christmass hearth to warm
He swings and twists his hazel band
And lops them off wi' sharpened hook
And oft brings ivy in his hand
To decorate the chimney nook

Old winter whipes his icles bye
And warms his fingers till he smiles
Where cottage hearths are blazing high
And labour resteth from his toils
Wi' merry mirth beguiling care
Old customs keeping wi' the day
Friends meet their Christmass cheer to share
And pass it in a harmless way

Old customs O I love the sound
However simple they may be
What ere with time has sanction found
Is welcome and is dear to me
Pride grows above simplicity
And spurns it from her haughty mind
And soon the poets song will be
The only refuge they can find

The shepherd now no more afraid
Since custom doth the chance bestow
Starts up to kiss the giggling maid
Beneath the branch of mizzletoe
That 'neath each cottage beam is seen
Wi' pearl-like berrys shining gay
The shadow still of what hath been
Which fashion yearly fades away

And singers too a merry throng
At early morn wi' simple skill
Yet imitate the angels' song
And chant their Christmass ditty still
And mid the storm that dies and swells
By fits-in humings softly steals
The music of the village bells
Ringing round their merry peals

And when it's past a merry crew
Bedeckt in masks and ribbons gay
The 'Morrice danse' their sports renew
And act their winter evening play
The clown-turnd-kings for penny praise
Storm wi' the actors strut and swell
And harlequin a laugh to raise
Wears his hump back and tinkling bell

And oft for pence and spicy ale
Wi' winter nosegays pind before
The wassail singer tells her tale
And drawls her Christmass carrols o'er
The prentice boy wi' ruddy face
And rhyme bepowder'd dancing locks
From door to door wi' happy pace
Runs round to claim his 'Christmass box'

The block behind the fire is put
To sanction customs old desires
And many a faggots bands are cut
For the old farmers Christmass fires
Where loud tong'd gladness joins the throng
And winter meets the warmth of May
Feeling by times the heat too strong
And rubs his shins and draws away

While snow the window panes bedim
The fire curls up a sunny charm
Where creaming o'er the pitchers rim
The flowering ale is set to warm
Mirth full of joy as summer bees
Sits there its pleasures to impart
While childern 'tween their parents knees
Sing scraps of carrols o'er by heart

And some to view the winter weathers
Climb up the window seat wi' glee
Likening the snow to falling feathers
In fancy's infant extacy
Laughing wi' superstitious love
O'er visions wild that youth supplyes
Of people pulling geese above
And keeping Christmass in the skyes

As tho' homestead trees were drest
In lieu of snow wi' dancing leaves
As tho' the sundryd martin's nest
Instead of icles hung the eaves
The children hail the happy day
As if the snow was April grass
And pleas'd as 'neath the warmth of May
Sport o'er the water froze to glass

Thou day of happy sound and mirth
That long wi' childish memory stays
How blest around the cottage hearth
I met thee in my boyish days
Harping wi' raptures dreaming joys
On presents that thy coming found
The welcome sight of little toys
The Christmass gifts of comers round

The wooden horse wi' arching head
Drawn upon wheels around the room
The gilded coach of ginger bread
And many color'd sugar plumb
Gilt cover'd books for pictures sought
Or storys childhood loves to tell
Wi' many a urgent promise bought
To get tomorrows lesson well

And many a thing a minutes sport
Left broken on the sanded floor
When we woud leave our play and court
Our parents promises for more
Tho' manhood bids such raptures dye
And throws such toys away as vain
Yet memory loves to turn her eye
And talk such pleasures o'er again

Around the glowing hearth at night
The harmless laugh and winter tale
Goes round while parting friends delight
To toast each other o'er their ale
The cotter oft wi' quiet zeal
Will musing o'er his Bible lean
While in the dark the lovers steal
To kiss and toy behind the screen

The Yule cake dotted thick wi' plumbs
Is on each supper table found
And cats look up for falling crumbs
Which greedy children litter round
And huswifes sage stuff'd season'd chine
Long hung in chimney nook to drye
And boiling eldern berry wine
To drink the Christmass Eve's 'good bye'

John Clare *The Shepherd's Calendar* **1827**

An effigy of a thirteenth-century Boy Bishop in Salisbury Cathedral

Bringing in the boar's head at Queen's College Oxford. This drawing
was made for the *Illustrated London News* by J. L. Williams in 1846

Decorating the church with evergreens: engraved after a drawing
by John Leech, 1869

CHAPTER V

21 DECEMBER,

ST THOMAS'S DAY

ST THOMAS'S DAY

The Traditions of St Thomas's Day

ST THOMAS was the patron saint of old people, so this was the day for giving them small presents of money to help them buy their Christmas food. Just in case anyone was forgotten, old people were allowed to ask for their money. This was called Thomasing, going a-gooding or mumping. St Thomas was also the patron saint of architects and builders, but it was probably thought that they could look after themselves because no one seems to have given them presents on the 21st.

The poor children of the parish also used to go round on St Thomas's Day to ask for corn for their frumenty, cakes, or sweets. Frumenty was a kind of porridge made from grains of wheat boiled in milk and then seasoned with sugar and cinnamon. Circulating round Warwickshire parishes was called 'going a-corning', after the special bags the children carried to put the corn in. As they toured round the village they would sing:

> Christmas is coming and the geese are getting fat,
> Please spare a penny for the old man's hat,
> If you haven't got a penny, a ha'penny will do,
> If you haven't got a ha'penny, God bless you.

Many St Thomas's Day customs existed in different versions throughout the country. In Worcestershire it was traditional for the children to ask for apples rather than corn. To help people part with their money, the Worcestershire children would sing:

> Wassail, wassail, through the town,
> If you've got any apples, throw them down;
> If you've got no apples, money will do;

The jug is white and the ale is brown,
This is the best house in the town.

Wassailing

Wassail, which is mentioned in the first line of the Worcestershire St Thomas's Day song, is a centuries-old toast which one still hears to this day at Christmas time. Like mistletoe, the Mummers plays and Father Christmas, it was a harmless pagan tradition which the Church did not try to stop. The word comes from the Anglo-Saxon *wes hal* meaning literally, 'be whole'. If someone said to you 'wassail', you replied 'drinkhail' which was the equivalent of 'your health'. There was a lot of 'wassailing' and 'drinkhailing' during the traditional celebration of Christmas. It was customary for every family to have a wassail bowl steaming away throughout the Christmas season. The traditional content of the wassail bowl was 'lamb's wool' which was made by mixing hot ale with the pulp of roasted apples and adding sugar and spices. The full recipe, supposedly as used in the kitchens of the court of Charles I, was: 'Boil three pints of ale; beat six eggs, the whites and yolks together; set both to the fire in a pewter pot; add roasted apples, sugar, beaten nutmegs, cloves and ginger; and, being well brewed, drink it while hot.'

In some parts of England it was the custom for singers to go from house to house with the wassail bowl decorated with ribbons, garlands, and sometimes a gilded apple. Arriving at each house, the singers would invite the householders to drink 'wassail' to the season and then top up the bowl. The song which accompanied this is similar to the Worcestershire St Thomas's Day song:

Wassail, wassail all over the town,
Our toast is white, our ale is brown,
Our bowl is made of a maplin tree;
We be good fellows all – I drink to thee.

Wassailing was fairly easily reconciled with the teachings of the Church. In fact it was a good promoter of 'peace and goodwill unto all men' but some of the traditions connected with the wassail bowl remained firmly pagan. On one of the evenings before Christmas in Hertfordshire, it was customary for everyone to wassail the oxen in their barn. If the ox had been 'toasted' as a reminder that it was one of the two animals beside the crib at the time of the Nativity, then this custom might have been acceptable to the Church, but the Hereford-shire method seems to have had little to do with religion. A cake with a hole through the middle was hung on the horns of the favourite ox. If the cake fell off when the ox tossed his head backwards, it went to the mistress of the house. If the cake fell off at a forward toss of the head, the cake went to the bailiff or chief farm hand. Presumably if the ox trod on it, the cake went to the priest.

Boars' Heads

A boar's head ceremony takes place every year at Queen's College Oxford on the Saturday before Christmas. The ceremony com-memorates a student of one of the colleges who once escaped from a boar in a highly original manner. He was walking in the nearby forest of Shotover, studying his Aristotle, when suddenly from the under-growth there rushed a wild boar of fearsome aspect. To avoid being gored to death by the boar's terrible tusks, the student thrust his copy of Aristotle down the beast's throat, explaining '*Graecum est*' ('It's in Greek'). During the college ceremony the chef bears in a boar's head on a silver salver with an orange between its teeth, and decked round with rosemary, bay and holly. The choir follows in behind the chef, singing:

> Caput apri defero *(I carry the boar's head)*
> Reddens laudes Domino. *(Giving praises to God.)*
> *The boar's head in hand bear I,*
> *With garlands gay and rosemary,*
> *I pray you all sing merrily*
> Qui estis in convivio. *(You who are at the banquet.)*

After the dish has reached the table, the orange is given to the chief singer and the sprigs of rosemary and bay to the guests.

Many other places celebrated Christmas with a boar's head; boar hunts were a popular Christmas sport in the Middle Ages. In Scandinavia, a boar's head was eaten in the Yuletide period in honour of the Sun-Boar and it was widely believed that the heroes in their great hall of Valhalla feasted perpetually on boar's flesh. The Celts believed that the boar was an agent of evil. The early Welsh legend of Culhwch and Olwen describes a hunt led by Arthur of Britain and his men in pursuit of the boar Trwyth. The Christian Church was quick to interpret legends such as this, and so the boar became symbolic of the powers of darkness, while Arthur symbolized those who fought the good fight. The Church also had a further, and rather curious, authority for permitting the pagan boar hunt to continue – Psalm 80:

> *Thou hast brought a vine out of Egypt:*
> *thou hast cast out the heathen, and planted it . . .*

why hast thou then broken down her hedge:
that all they that go by pluck off her grapes?
The wild boar out of the wood doth root it up:
and the wild beasts of the field devour it.

Any wild boar incautious enough to root up a nobleman's vine in the Middle Ages was liable to end up on a silver salver with an orange in its mouth.

At Hornchurch in Essex, the man who had the lease of the parish tithes each year had to provide a dressed and garnished boar's head. One afternoon before Christmas it was carried into the field next to the churchyard and the men of the village wrestled for possession of it. The man who won it took it off to the pub and then had a feast with his friends.

A much grander boar's head feast was one held at the court of James I:

The first messe was a Boar's Head, which was carried by the tallest and lustiest of all the guard, before whom (as attendants) went one attired in a horseman's coat, with a boar's speare in his hande, next to him another Huntsman in greene, with a bloody faulcion drawn, next to him two Pages in tafatye sarcanet, each of them with a messe of mustard; next to whom came hee who carried the Boar's head crost with a green silk scarf, by which hunge the empty scabbard of the faulcion which was carried before him.

They sang:

The Boar is dead,
Loe, here is his head,
What man could have done more
Than his head off to strike,
Meleager like,
And bring it as I do before?
He livinge spoyled
Where good men toyled,
Which made king Ceres sorrye;
But now dead and drawne,
Is very good brawne,
And we have brought it for you.
Then set down the Swineyard,
The foe to the Vineyard,
Let Bacchus crown his fall,
Let this Boar's head and mustard
Stand for Pigg, goose and Custard,
And so you are wellcom all.

CHRISTMAS WITH THE POOTERS

The Diary of a Nobody first appeared in Punch *in the 1890s and was published in book form in 1894. It was written by two actor brothers, George and Weedon Grossmith. In diary form, it tells of the doings – almost non-doings – of Mr Pooter and his family, who are upper-lower-middle class, or lower-middle-middle class, and live extremely ordinary lives in an ordinary house, with ordinary people about them. It has become a classic of humour because of the diarist's, Mr Pooter's, rather pompous innocence and the clear picture it gives of late-Victorian bourgeois life. In this first extract we move upwards in the social scale from John Clare and see how the family of a 'senior clerk in a mercantile establishment' prepares for Christmas.*

DECEMBER 19:

The annual invitation came to spend Christmas with Carrie's mother – the usual family festive gathering to which we always look forward. Lupin declined to go. I was astounded, and expressed my surprise and disgust. Lupin then obliged us with the following Radical speech: 'I hate a family gathering at Christmas. What does it mean? Why, someone says: "Ah! we miss poor Uncle James, who was here last year," and we all begin to snivel. Someone else says: "It's two years since poor Aunt Liz used to sit in that corner." Then we all begin to snivel again. Then another gloomy relation says: "Ah! I wonder whose turn it will be next?" Then we all snivel again, and proceed to eat and drink too much; and they don't discover until I get up that we have been seated thirteen at dinner.'

DECEMBER 20:

Went to Smirksons', the drapers, in the Strand, who this year have turned out everything in the shop and devoted the whole place to the sale of Christmas cards. Shop crowded with people, who seemed to take up the cards rather roughly, and, after a hurried glance at them, throw them down again. I remarked to one of the persons serving that carelessness appeared to be a disease with some purchasers. The observation was scarcely out of my mouth, when my thick coat-sleeve caught against a large pile of expensive cards in boxes one on top of the other, and threw them down. The manager came forward, looking very much annoyed, and picking up several cards from the ground, said to one of the assistants, with a palpable side-glance at me: 'Put these amongst the sixpenny goods, they can't be sold for a shilling now.' The result was, I felt it my duty to buy some of these damaged cards. I had to buy more and pay more than intended. Unfortunately I did not examine them all, and when I got home I discovered a vulgar card with a picture of a fat nurse with two babies, one black and the other white, and the words: 'We wish Pa a Merry Christmas.' I tore up the card and threw it away.

DECEMBER 21:

To save the postman a miserable Christmas, we follow the example of all unselfish people, and send out our cards early. Most of the cards had finger-marks, which I did not notice at night. I shall buy all future cards in the daytime. Lupin (who, ever since he has had the appointment with a stock and share broker, does not seem overscrupulous in his dealings) told me never to rub out the pencilled price on the backs of the cards. I asked him why. Lupin said: 'Suppose your card is marked 9d. Well, all you have to do is to pencil a 3 – and a long down-stroke after it – in *front* of the ninepence, and people will think you have given five times the price for it.'

DECEMBER 24:

I am a poor man, but I would gladly give ten shillings to find out who sent me the insulting Christmas card I received this morning. I never insult people; why should they insult me? The worst part of the transaction is, that I find myself suspecting all my friends. The handwriting on the envelope is evidently disguised, being written sloping the wrong way. I cannot think either Gowing or Cummings would do such a mean thing. Lupin denied all knowledge of it, and I believe him; although I disapprove of his laughing and sympathizing with the offender. Mr Franching would be above such an act; and I don't think any of the Mutlars would descend to such a course. I wonder if Pitt, that impudent clerk at the office, did it? Or Mrs Birrell, the charwoman, or Burwin-Fosselton? The writing is too good for the former.

George and Weedon Grossmith *The Diary of a Nobody* **1894**

CHAPTER VI

24 DECEMBER,

CHRISTMAS EVE

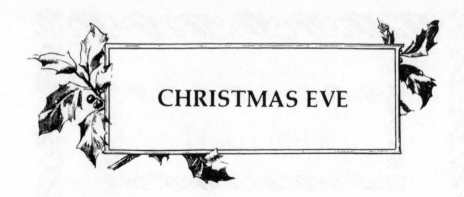

CHRISTMAS EVE

The Yule Log

THE MOST important event of Christmas Eve was the hauling in of the Yule log. The seventeenth-century poet, Robert Herrick, described the excitement of this:

> Come, bring with a noise,
> My merrie, merrie boyes,
> The Christmas Log to the firing;
> While my good Dame, she
> Bids ye all be free;
> And drink to your hearts desiring.
>
> With the last yeeres brand
> Light the new block, and
> For good success in his spending,
> On your Psaltries play,
> That sweet luck may
> Come while the log is a-tending.
>
> Drink now the strong Beere,
> Cut the white loafe here,
> The while the meat is a-shredding;
> For the rare Mince-Pie
> And the Plums stand by
> To fill the paste that's a-kneading.

A log of the right size and imposing shape was carefully selected, trimmed, and perhaps dragged for a considerable distance through mud, slush and snow by willing hands, smallish children being allowed to ride astride it. Once inside it was rolled on to the fire to burn throughout the vigil of the Nativity and on through Christmas Day. For a great house with a large fireplace, an enormous log – half a tree-trunk – would be used and left to smoulder right through till Twelfth Night.

The ceremony of the Yule log, like so many of the oldest Christmas traditions, was thoroughly pagan in origin. The Norsemen made a habit of burning logs of oak in honour of the god Thor (who gave his name to Thursday), and the ancient Celtic belief in the sacredness of perpetual fire led to the old English tradition that the log had to be lit from a brand left over from the previous year's log. Primitive man had always associated fire with warmth and life, and the burning log at Christmas, at the height of the cold, lifeless winter months, was symbolic of the undying sun which was soon to bring spring and fruitfulness back to the earth.

The Church attempted to give the Yule log some Christian significance by putting it about that the log should be ash. This was because the infant Jesus was first washed and dressed alongside an ash fire, which the shepherds had made. They had used ash because they had to make the fire at a moment's notice and ash is the only wood which will burn while it is still green, without spluttering as pine does. It became the traditional wood for the Yule log in England. In Scotland the Yule log was often a length of birch tree stripped of its bark, which gave rise to the proverb: 'He's as bare as a bark on Yule e'en' (i.e. he's very poor).

Despite the Church's attempt to impose Christian traditions on to the Yule log, the widely held opinion that it was unlucky to let the fire go out was another throwback to the Celtic belief in the sacredness of perpetual fire. In fact it was unlucky to let any kind of fire go out over Christmas; and equally unlucky to go round to your neighbour for a light. To avoid the embarrassment and ill omens should this ever happen, some towns and villages kept a communal bonfire alight throughout the Christmas period. It was also a superstition that the fire would burn badly if a maid did not wash her hands before touching the log. Bad luck too, should a squinting or barefoot person come into the house while the Yule log was burning. Finally, if anybody threw the ashes out of the house on Christmas Day, it was thought that they would be throwing them in the face of Christ. Nevertheless, if you avoided doing this the ashes were thought to have magical properties. They were strongly recommended as a cure for toothache, to rid cattle of vermin, to give the ground added fertility and to protect the house from fire and ill luck.

The arrival of the Yule log inside the house on Christmas Eve was always an opportunity for a small celebration. *The Baron's Yule Feast – a Christmas Rhyme*, written by the Chartist poet Thomas Cooper in 1846, describes one such:

They pile the Yule-log on the hearth,
Soak toasted crabs in ale;
And while they sip, their homely mirth
Is joyous as if all the earth
For man were void of bale.

The crabs toasted in ale were not the seaside sort, but crab apples, or any sort of wild apple.

On the Continent too, the custom of the Yule log played a part in traditional celebrations of Christmas; particularly in France and parts of Germany. The French Christmas cake, a *bûche de Noël*, is an imitation log made with chocolate icing.

A COUNTRY PARSON'S CHRISTMAS EVE

THURSDAY, CHRISTMAS EVE 1874

Writing Christmas letters all the morning. In the afternoon
I went to the church with Dora and Teddy to put up
Christmas decorations. Dora had been very busy for some
days past making the straw letters for the Christmas text.
Fair Rosamund and good Elizabeth Knight came to the
church to help us and worked heartily and well. They had
made some pretty ivy knots and bunches for the pulpit panels
and the ivy blossoms cleverly whitened with flour looked
just like white flowers.

The churchwarden Jacob Knight was sitting by his sister
in front of the roaring fire. We were talking of the death of
Major Torrens on the ice at Corsham pond yesterday.
Speaking of people slipping and falling on ice the good
churchwarden sagely remarked, 'Some do fall on their faces
and some do fall on their rumps. And they as do hold their
selves uncommon stiff do most in generally fall on
their rumps.'

I took old John Bryant a Christmas packet of tea and
sugar and raisins from my Mother. The old man had covered
himself almost entirely over in his bed to keep himself warm,
like a marmot in its nest. He said, 'If I live till New Year's Day
I shall have seen ninety-six New Years.' He said also,
'I do often see things flying about me, thousands and
thousands of them about half the size of a large pea, and they
are red, white, blue, and yellow and all colours. I asked
Mr Morgan what they were and he said they were the
spirits of just men made perfect.'

The Rev. Francis Kilvert *Diary 1870-1879*

Dumb Cakes

While the men were tugging home the Yule log, the women were preparing the food for Christmas Day, but they did have a traditional dish for Christmas Eve as well. This was the Dumb Cake, which was made by single girls who wanted to know who their husbands were going to be. The recipe, which still survives in Northamptonshire, describes taking 'an eggshellful of salt, another of wheatmeal and a third of barley'. The point was for the girl to make the cake in absolute silence and on her own. After she had made the cake and put it in the oven, she opened the door of the house and, if all went well, her future husband would walk in at midnight and turn the cake.

In the Cotswolds the cook pricked her initials on the top of the cake, put it in the oven, then opened the front door and waited. At midnight her intended would walk in and prick his initials next to hers. Then she would eat the cake.

Christmas Decorations

In the past, a house which observed the old traditional Christmas would probably have been decked out with holly, ivy and mistletoe long before Christmas Eve. If it had not already been decorated then Christmas Eve was the last opportunity.

The tradition of bringing holly and ivy, or any evergreen, into the house is another Christmas practice which goes back to the Romans. Bringing evergreens home and presenting branches to people was a custom in Rome during the winter celebrations; evergreen was a token of good luck. But it was relatively easy for the Church to make holly a Christian symbol. Its needle-sharp leaves and blood-red berries became associated with Christ's crown of thorns. Ivy was much more difficult because it had been the badge of the deeply pagan Bacchus, the Roman god of wine. Nevertheless, the customs and superstitions associated with holly and ivy, like the Yule log, had really nothing to do with Christianity at all.

In medieval Christmas songs, holly is often sung of as man's plant, while ivy represents woman; rivalry follows, as in the fifteenth-century song:

> Holver and Heivy made a grete party,
> Who should have the maistry
> In londès where they go.

In the Midlands, the tradition was that if the first holly to be brought into the house at Christmas was prickly, the master would rule for the coming year; if the holly was smooth-leaved, then the mistress would rule. Holly was also thought to be hateful to witches, and therefore good luck to the householder. In the west of England girls were recommended to decorate their beds with berried holly to ward off goblins.

Richard Steele, writing in his periodical the *Spectator* at the beginning of the eighteenth century, passed comment on the custom of bringing large quantities of evergreen into the church at Christmas time. He wrote a letter under the name of Jenny Simper, who complained:

> I am a young Woman, and have my fortune to make, for which reason I come constantly to Church to hear Divine Service, and make Conquests; but one great Hindrance in this my design is, that our Clerk, who was once a Gardener, has this Christmas so over-decked the Church with Greens, that he has quite spoiled my prospect, insomuch that I have scarce seen the young Baronet I dress at these last three Weeks, though we have both been very Constant at our Devotions, and do not sit above three Pews off. The Church, as it is now equipped, looks more like a Greenhouse than a Place of Worship; the middle Isle is a very pretty Shady Walk, and the Pews look like so many Arbours on each side of it. The Pulpit itself has such Clusters of Ivy, Holly, and Rosemary about it, that a light Fellow in our Pew took Occasion to say, that The Congregation heard the Word out of a Bush, like Moses.

Mistletoe

Mistletoe was always known to have played an important part in the rituals of the Druids and, consequently, it was never really accepted by the Church. York Minster was the only church exempt from the rule that mistletoe was not to be used in church decoration. There, each Christmas, a bough of mistletoe was brought in by the clergy and laid on the altar; then 'a public liberty, pardon and freedom to all sorts of inferior and even wicked people at the gates of the city to the four corners of the earth' was proclaimed.

The Arch Druid was supposed to have cut the mistletoe with a golden sickle around November each year. It was caught as it fell from the tree by virgins holding out a white cloth. There then followed prayer and the sacrifice of white oxen, which were popularly thought to have replaced human sacrifices. The mistletoe was then divided up amongst the people, who took it home to hang over their doors. It was held to work miracles of healing, to protect against witchcraft, and to bring fertility to the land and the people of the house.

Kissing under the mistletoe is peculiar to Britain and the origins of the custom are unknown. It may have had something to do with the Druidical belief in its powers of fertility. The traditional form of the custom was that each time a kiss was claimed under the bough, the young men picked off a berry; when all the berries were gone there was no more kissing.

The Christmas Tree

Christmas today is hardly complete without a Christmas tree. Take or, more legally, buy one small fir tree, preferably pre-sprayed to prevent all its needles falling off. Shove into plastic bucket normally used for washing car and now decorated with the local paper sprayed silver and wrapped round it. Struggle for three quarters of an hour trying to get the tree to stand upright in wet soil on loan from the kitchen garden. Spend the rest of Christmas Eve decorating the tree with gaudily coloured celluloid globes, two hundred feet of electric flex and enough coloured lights to eclipse Blackpool. Collapse tearfully into armchair as the dogs, overexcited at having stolen the insides of the turkey, skate into the electric flex, fuse the lights, break the coloured balls and fell the tree.

In fact, in England the tradition of a tree at Christmas is only about a hundred and forty years old. Before that it was an almost entirely German tradition. Some authorities maintain that its origins lay in the pagan worship of vegetation, the same worship that led to the symbolism of the Mummers plays and the tradition of decorating the house with holly and ivy. Others associate it with the story of St Boniface, an English missionary in Germany during the eighth century also known as St Boniface of Crediton. One Christmas Eve in Germany, he was said to have chopped down a sacred oak beneath which human sacrifices had been offered. As the oak fell, a young fir tree miraculously appeared in its place. Because of this, the saint suggested the fir tree as an emblem of the new faith he had brought to Germany. Combined with this there was a legend, first told by Georg Jacob, a tenth-century geographer, that on the night Christ was born all the trees in the forest, despite the fact that it was mid-winter, bloomed and bore fruit.

A German custom linked with this legend was the bringing indoors of cherry, pear or hawthorn boughs and putting them in water so that they blossomed at Christmas time. The Germans also believed that Martin Luther first decorated the Christmas tree. The story goes that he was walking one Christmas Eve under a clear night sky lit by millions of stars, and the sight so moved him that when he returned home he took with him an uprooted fir tree and fixed candles to its branches to remind children of the heavens from which Christ descended to save us. By 1604, decorating fir trees had become fairly common practice. A

Celebrating Christmas Eve, a cartoon by George Cruikshank for a *Comic Almanack*

Two Christmas scenes engraved by Robert Seymour in 1836: *above* the Norfolk coech arriving in London laden with turkeys; *below* a traditional Christmas dinner

The Christmas tree at Windsor Castle in 1848. Queen Victoria and her mother, the Duchess of Kent, stand to the left, and the Prince Consort to the right, while five of the royal children admire their presents

German writing in that year described it thus: 'At Christmas they set up fir trees in the parlours of Strasbourg and hang thereon roses cut out of many-coloured paper, apples, wafers, gold foil, sweets etc.'

It is generally believed that Prince Albert introduced the Christmas tree into England in 1841 but there were Christmas trees in England about ten years before that. A German, Princess Lieven, had one put up for Christmas 1829; the nineteenth-century diarist, Charles Greville, recorded in his memoirs: 'It was very pretty. Here it was only for the children; in Germany the custom extends to persons of all ages.' What Queen Victoria and her husband did do was to popularize the tree as the central feature of a family Christmas. Of her own Christmas tree at Windsor, Queen Victoria wrote in 1841: 'Today I have two children of my own to give presents to, who, they know not why, are full of happy wonder at the German Christmas tree and its radiant candles.' This German custom, together with sounding trumpets at the New Year 'quite affected dear Albert who turned pale, and had tears in his eyes, and pressed my hand very warmly'.

DICKENS'S CHRISTMAS TREE

I have been looking on, this evening, at a merry company of children assembled round that pretty German toy, a Christmas tree. The tree was planted in the middle of a great round table, and towered high above their heads. It was brilliantly lighted by a multitude of little tapers; and everywhere sparkled and glittered with bright objects. There were rosy-cheeked dolls, hiding behind the green leaves; and there were real watches (with movable hands, at least, and an endless capacity of being wound up) dangling from innumerable twigs; there were French-polished tables, chairs, bedsteads, wardrobes, eight-day clocks, and various other articles of domestic furniture (wonderfully made, in tin, at Wolverhampton), perched among the boughs, as if in preparation for some fairy housekeeping; there were jolly, broad-faced men, much more agreeable in appearance than many real men – and no wonder, for their heads took off, and showed them to be full of sugar-plums; there were fiddles and drums; there were tambourines, books, work-boxes, paint-boxes, sweetmeat boxes, peep-show boxes, and all kinds of boxes; there were trinkets for the elder girls, far brighter than any grown-up gold and jewels; there were baskets and pin-cushions in all devices; there were guns, swords and banners; there were witches standing in enchanted rings of pasteboard, to tell fortunes; there were tetotums, humming-tops, needle-cases, pen-wipers, smelling-bottles, conversation-cards, bouquet-holders; real fruit, made artificially dazzling with gold leaf; imitation apples, pears, and walnuts, crammed with surprises; in short, as a pretty child, before me, delightfully whispered to another pretty child, her bosom friend, 'There was everything, and more.'

Charles Dickens 'A Christmas Tree' in *Household Words* **1850**

The Kissing Bough

In his book *The English Festivals* (London, 1947), the poet and glass-engraver Laurence Whistler has shown that in many parts of rural England there was an alternative to the Christmas tree called a kissing bough. This was a spherical framework bound with box, rosemary or some other evergreen, inside which red apples dangled from coloured ribbons. Fixed to the strip of metal or osier that formed the circumference of the sphere were coloured candles. The whole thing was then hung up in a prominent place and mistletoe tied beneath it.

One year our family decided that a kissing bough might be more fun than the usual tree. Out came the pliers and the wire. Simple craftsmanship. As we did not grow either box or rosemary in the garden we chose pagan ivy. This we bound round the wire frame. Next came the seven apples suspended on red ribbons. So far no problems, but where to put it? The hall ceiling was too low to hang a four-foot round, verdant football. The answer seemed to be to hang it above the staircase. This entailed climbing a ladder, chiselling the paint out of the joints on the outside of the window overlooking the stairs, and then pushing a five-foot length of wood through the gap between the bottom of the window and the frame. Inside, this piece of wood stuck out over the stairs like a gibbet. Next we threw up some nylon washing line with a guaranteed breaking-strain of half a ton – essential for our kissing bough – and hauled the mighty structure up into position. With the aid of a step-ladder the candles were fixed on. The village shop had run out of the little red ones so we had to make do with the leftovers from last year's power cuts. Once lit, it looked really rather Christmassy. We all stood round and watched the candlelight reflecting off the red apples and the draught from the partly opened window blowing the drips of wax on to the dogs. What better way of celebrating Christmas Eve than picking wax out of Afghan hound coats?

The Crib

The idea of having a model version of the Nativity came from St Francis of Assisi. Another saint, St Bonaventure, writing in the thirteenth century, describes how St Francis hit upon the idea:

> *That this might not seem an innovation, he sought and obtained licence from the supreme pontiff, and they made ready a manger, and bade hay, together with an ox and an ass, be brought unto the place . . . The man of God (St Francis) filled with tender love, stood before the manager, bathed in tears, and overflowing with joy. Solemn masses were celebrated over the manger, Francis the Levite of Christ chanting the Holy Gospel.*

After Christmas the hay that had been in the crib 'proved a marvellous remedy for sick beasts, and prophylactic against divers other plagues'. The crib was also called a 'manger', after the French verb meaning 'to eat'. Before a century had passed most of Europe had cribbed the crib. Carved sets were available dressed in contemporary styles. This presented no problem if the Three Wise Men were dressed as the kings of the day, and there was no real difference in dress between a fifteenth-century shepherd and the shepherds of the Bible. The whole thing became more complicated in the seventeenth century, when the angels were given powdered wigs and wide-brimmed hats with feather trimmings.

The Old Lad's Passing Bell

While the spinsters of the parishes of England were silently preparing their dumb cakes and the young men were shuffling about in the cold outside, waiting for the moment when they could nip in and thumb their initials into the cakes, the church bell would begin to toll. On the three mornings before Christmas, peals were rung to remind everyone that Christmas was coming. One cannot help feeling that if the people of rural England followed a third of the customs described here they were in no danger at all of forgetting what time of year it was. The bell that tolled from eleven till midnight, 'The Old Lad's Passing Bell', tolled for the death of the devil and the approaching birth of Christ. Perhaps the nick-name was rather too affectionate — the custom was forbidden after the Reformation.

A VISIT FROM ST NICHOLAS

The most famous Christmas poem of the last hundred and fifty years,
particularly to American children, was this jolly story of St Nicholas's
arrival down the chimney with his sack of toys on his back. It was written
by a classical scholar, Clement Clarke Moore, who was the professor of
Greek at a New York Theological Seminary.

'Twas the night before Christmas, when all through the house
Not a creature was stirring, not even a mouse;
The stockings were hung by the chimney with care,
In hopes that St Nicholas soon would be there;
The children were nestled all snug in their beds,
While visions of sugar-plums danced in their heads;
And mamma in her 'kerchief, and I in my cap,
Had just settled our brains for a long winter's nap,
When out on the lawn there arose such a clatter,
I sprang from the bed to see what was the matter.
Away to the window I flew like a flash,
Tore open the shutters and threw up the sash.
The moon on the breast of the new-fallen snow
Gave the lustre of mid-day to objects below,
When, what to my wondering eyes should appear,
But a miniature sleigh, and eight tiny reindeer,
With a little old driver, so lively and quick,
I knew in a moment it must be St Nick.
More rapid than eagles his coursers they came,
And he whistled, and shouted, and called them by name;
'Now Dasher! now, Dancer! now, Prancer and Vixen!
On, Comet! on, Cupid! on, Donner and Blitzen!
To the top of the porch! to the top of the wall!
Now dash away! dash away! dash away all!'
As dry leaves that before the wild hurricane fly,
When they meet with an obstacle, mount to the sky;
So up to the house-top the coursers they flew,
With the sleigh full of toys, and St Nicholas too.
And then, in a twinkling, I heard on the roof
The prancing and pawing of each little hoof.
As I drew in my head, and was turning around,
Down the chimney St Nicholas came with a bound.
He was dressed all in fur, from his head to his foot,
And his clothes were all tarnished with ashes and soot.

A bundle of toys he had flung on his back,
And he looked like a pedlar, just opening his pack.
His eyes - how they twinkled! his dimples how merry!
His cheeks were like roses, his nose like a cherry!
His droll little mouth was drawn up like a bow,
And the beard of his chin was as white as the snow;
The stump of a pipe he held tight in his teeth,
And the smoke it encircled his head like a wreath;
He had a broad face and a little round belly,
That shook when he laughed, like a bowlful of jelly.
He was chubby and plump, a right jolly old elf,
And I laughed when I saw him, in spite of myself;
A wink of his eye and a twist of his head,
Soon gave me to know I had nothing to dread.
He spoke not a word, but went straight to his work,
And filled all the stockings; then turned with a jerk,
And laying his finger aside of his nose,
And giving a nod, up the chimney he rose;
He sprang to his sleigh, to his team gave a whistle,
And away they all flew like the down of a thistle.
But I heard him exclaim, 'ere he drove out of sight,
'Happy Christmas to all, and to all a good-night.'

Clement Clark Moore (1779-1863) *The Night Before Christmas*

CHAPTER VII

25 DECEMBER,

CHRISTMAS DAY

CHRISTMAS DAY

Midnight Mass

TRADITIONALLY, the celebrations of Christmas Day began with midnight mass on Christmas Eve. This mass was always special, even for people who usually found going to church every Sunday something of a chore. The Church made little attempt to exclude the pagan spirit of Christmas fun from the Christmas midnight mass and people would be marvelling at the decorations, admiring each other's new clothes and calling out 'Happy Christmas!' across the aisle.

Superstitions were theoretically frowned upon by the Church as being beliefs arising from ignorance. However, in the Middle Ages, when so much of nature seemed inexplicable even to the Church, many simple superstitions were permitted as long as they did not conflict with the Church's teachings. There were a whole host of superstitions about midnight on Christmas Eve.

People thought that animals celebrated the arrival of Christ and that the cows in the cattle-sheds and the deer in the forests went down on their knees at midnight. Thomas Hardy wrote a poem about this:

'Christmas Eve, and twelve of the clock,
Now they are all on their knees,'
An elder said as we sat in a flock
By the embers in the hearthside ease.

We pictured the meek mild creatures where
They dwelt in their strawy pen,
Nor did it occur to one of us there
To doubt they were kneeling then.

So fair a fancy few would weave
In these years! Yet, I feel,

If someone said on Christmas Eve,
'Come; see the oxen kneel

In the lonely barton by yonder coomb
Our children used to know',
I should go with him in the gloom,
Hoping it might be so.

Bees, too, were supposed to celebrate the Nativity by waking up from their winter sleep and humming a song of praise to Christ. Unfortunately, only those who had led a blameless life could hope to hear those Beatitudes. Animals were able to speak like humans, or so it was widely believed; they must have spoken in Latin, and too fast, because we have no record of what they said. Not to be outdone by the animal kingdom, the trees and plants along the banks of the River Jordan bowed in reverence at midnight.

Ghosts, witches and other evil creatures of the night all had their powers suspended. Shakespeare knew about this because he wrote in *Hamlet*:

Some say that ever 'gainst that season comes
Wherein our Saviour's birth is celebrated,
The bird of dawning singeth all night long;
And then they say, no spirit dare walk abroad.
The nights are wholesome; then no planets strike,
No fairy takes, nor witch hath power to charm –
So hallowed and so gracious is the time.

It was also a lucky time for good spirits. The Irish believed that the gates of Paradise were opened on the hour of midnight, so that if anyone should die at this time they would go straight up into heaven.

There were two sinister traditions too. If, when all were seated round the fire, one shadow on the wall behind was headless, then the person who cast the shadow would be dead before the end of the year. Someone would also die if a hoop fell off a cask on Christmas Eve. Not everyone was overjoyed that Christmas was upon them. On two Christmas Days a Somerset rector, John Skinner, wrote:

Thursday, 25 December 1823: I cannot say my sleep was disturbed, but my waking hours certainly were by the ringing of bells about seven o'clock announcing the joyous day, when half the parish at least would be drunk. Tuesday, 25 December 1827: I was awakened early by the ringing of the bells, and could not help thinking how much sound overpowers common sense in all that we have to do on the present day. I lay awake last night thinking of these things, and soon after I had closed my eyes they were again opened by the loud peals these thoughtless people among whom I dwell chose to ring, as they suppose, in honour of the day. They had better retire within themselves, and commune with their hearts, and be still.

Sowen Cakes and Candles

Before dawn on Christmas morning the Scots used to be up and about, baking cakes called sowens. These were made by boiling the farinaceous matter from the husks of oats and then forming the result into cakes. The liquid was drained off and drunk at Hogmanay. One was given to each member of the family who had to keep it unbroken till the big feast in the evening. If it did not break, then happiness would come to its owner. If the sowen broke, then any such happiness crumbled away with the cake.

The English had a similar custom concerning candles. The symbolism behind the tradition of the Christmas candle is that it represented the star of Bethlehem. Nevertheless, Christmas time also coincides with the ancient Jewish festival of Hanuca, the Feast of Lights. The Christian Church probably took over the candles from this earlier festival. Large candles were made at Christmas ready to be lit first thing on Christmas morning. As with the Scots, if the Christmas candle burnt out before the day was over this was a prophecy of bad times to come. Christmas candles were given as presents by grocers and chandlers to their regular customers.

A COLD CHRISTMAS DAY MORNING

SUNDAY, CHRISTMAS DAY 1870
As I lay awake praying in the early morning I thought I heard a sound of distant bells. It was an intense frost. I sat down in my bath upon a sheet of thick ice which broke in the middle into large pieces whilst sharp points and jagged edges stuck all round the sides of the tub like *chevaux de frise*, not particularly comforting to the naked thighs and loins, for the keen ice cut like broken glass. The ice water stung and scorched like fire. I had to collect the floating pieces of ice and pile them on a chair before I could use the sponge and then I had to thaw the sponge in my hands for it was a mass of ice. The morning was most brilliant. Walked to the Sunday School with Gibbins and the road sparkled with millions of rainbows, the seven colours gleaming in every glittering point of hoar frost. The church was very cold in spite of two roaring stove fires . . .

The Rev. Francis Kilvert *Diary 1870-1879*

Christmas Food

There was never a traditional time for eating Christmas food, lunch-time, tea-time or dinner-time serving just as well. The tradition of eating turkey goes back a long way. The first reference to turkey as the principal course in the Christmas dinner came during Henry VIII's reign. Before that a good Christmas meal was one with a wide choice of things to eat. The 'feast' was in eating as many different types of food as could be afforded. Most people could probably manage a choice of fish, goose or chicken; the rich had a much wider choice. One Christmas the court of Henry V offered, amongst other things, brawn and mustard, pike in erbage (herb-stuffed), powdered lamprey (small, salted, eel-like fish), jelly coloured with columbine flowers, bream, conger, salmon, roach, halibut, crayfish, lobster, sturgeon and whelks, roasted porpoise, carp, tench, turbot, perch and so on through the forty-odd species of freshwater fish, followed by marchpane garnished with angels (marchpane was the fore-runner of marzipan, a paste made from almonds and sugar, and the angels were only decorations; rather as angel cake is not normally made from real angels). But whether you were rich or poor, you made as good a show as you could.

An Elizabethan, Philip Massinger, passed comment on town and country appetites: 'Men may talk of country Christmasses – their thirty-pound buttered eggs, their pies of carps' tongues, their pheasants drenched with ambergris [ambergris is a secretion which comes from the stomach of the sperm whale. In the Middle Ages it was a prized ingredient in cooking; today it is used as a binding agent for scents], the carcases of three fat wethers [castrated rams] bruised for gravy to make sauce for a single peacock; yet their feasts were fasts, compared with the city's.'

MR POOTER MAKES A CHRISTMAS SPEECH

CHRISTMAS DAY

We caught the 10.20 train at Paddington, and spent a pleasant day at Carrie's mother's. The country was quite nice and pleasant, although the roads were sloppy. We dined in the middle of the day, just ten of us, and talked over old times. If everybody had a nice, *uninterfering* mother-in-law, such as I have, what a deal of happiness there would be in the world. Being all in good spirits, I proposed her health; and I made, I think, a very good speech.

I concluded, rather neatly, by saying: 'On such an occasion as this – whether relatives, friends, or acquaintances – we are all inspired with good feelings towards each other. We are of one mind, and think only of love and friendship. Those who have quarrelled with absent friends should kiss and make it up. Those who happily have *not* fallen out, can kiss all the same.'

I saw tears in the eyes of both Carrie and her mother, and must say I felt very flattered by the compliment. That dear old Reverend John Panzy Smith, who married us, made a most cheerful and amusing speech, and said he should act on my suggestion respecting the kissing. He then walked round the table and kissed all the ladies, including Carrie. Of course one did not object to this; but I was more than staggered when a young fellow named Moss, who was a stranger to me, and who had scarcely spoken a word through dinner, jumped up suddenly with a sprig of mistletoe, and exclaimed: 'Hulloh! I don't see why I shouldn't be on in this scene.' Before one could realise what he was about to do, he kissed Carrie and the rest of the ladies. Fortunately the matter was treated as a joke, and we all laughed; but it was a dangerous experiment, and I felt very uneasy for a moment as to the result. I subsequently referred to the matter to Carrie, but she said: 'Oh, he's not much more than a boy.' I said that he had a very large moustache for a boy. Carrie replied: 'I didn't say he was not a nice boy.'

George and Weedon Grossmith *The Diary of a Nobody* **1894**

The Christmas Turkey

Despite furious advertising by the turkey farmers, the only time most people eat turkey is at Christmas. Though this may seem lunatic to the farmers, it is only an old custom surviving. The tradition of eating turkey only at Christmas is a distant memory of the days when the principal dish on that day was something special. Before turkey took over, the popular Christmas delicacies were bustard, goose, and cockerel, and in the houses of the rich, peacock and swan. The peacock was often skinned before roasting. For serving it was reclothed in its feathers and its beak was gilded. Sometimes the beak was propped open with a bit of bread soaked in spirit. This would then be set on fire and the bird brought into the dining hall with the greatest pomp and ceremony.

J. A. Brillat-Savarin, the great French philosopher and historian of the kitchen, took considerable pains to prove that the Jesuits were responsible for first importing the turkey into Europe and breeding it over here in large numbers. In fact, the turkey was introduced into Europe by one of Sebastian Cabot's officers on a return journey from the New World, which is where the birds came from. They were called turkeys in England because merchants from the Levant, or Turkey, first brought them over here. Brillat-Savarin refuted the argument, once popular, that the Romans had enjoyed eating turkeys and that they had been presented as the main dish at Charlemagne's wedding feast, by the aristocratic reminder that this was almost certainly impossible because of 'the appearance of the bird, which is clearly outlandish'.

Turkeys were to Norfolk as boots were to Northants. By the end of the eighteenth century, Norwich alone was sending a thousand turkeys a day up to London, and the Norfolk turkey was the Rolls-Royce of birds.

Charles Lamb had this to say when he wrote to a friend who had the misfortune to be spending the Christmas of 1815 in China: 'You have no turkeys; you would not desecrate the festival by offering up a withered Chinese bantam instead of the savoury grand Norfolcian holocaust that smokes all around my nostrils at this moment from a thousand firesides.'

The questioning age in which we live, having swiped out at God and the monarchy, has even levelled criticism at the 'grand Norfolcian holocaust'. Of the turkey, William Connor, Cassandra of the *Daily Mirror*, wrote: 'What a shocking fraud the turkey is. In life preposterous, insulting – that foolish noise they make to scare you away! In death – unpalatable. The turkey has practically no taste except a dry fibrous flavour reminiscent of a mixture of warmed-up plaster of Paris and horsehair.'

Christmas Pudding

After the turkey, the Christmas pudding, maturing away in its bowl since Stir Up Sunday. The Christmas pudding should be brought in aflame, and this is how to do it. Avoid four-star Cognac; One-star, or motor-mower, brandy is the stuff; or, if you can make it burn, inexpensive brandy mixed fifty-fifty with cheap sherry. Check supplies before the shops shut on Christmas Eve.

The brandy must be warm – very important – otherwise the cold fluid soaks into the pudding, making it unsuitable for children and aged grannies. Heat a ladle or large spoon over the gas. Switch off gas. Pour brandy into ladle. Watch it hiss. Pour warm brandy over pud. Be careful how much you pour on: too much and the whole thing becomes a fireball scorching the paintwork on the ceiling. The flaming brandy is for display purposes only; most of it has been burnt away by the time you come to eat it, leaving the outside of the pudding slightly charred.

There is often a peculiarly bitter taste. That is what burnt holly tastes like.

THE DEFOSSILIZED PLUM PUDDING

At the beginning of the century literary parody was a favourite
form of humour among men of letters, the custom only dying out in the
1930s. For the Christmas Supplement of The Saturday Review
for Christmas, 1896, Max Beerbohm wrote a little story parodying
the literary style of H. G. Wells.

'Have some more of that stuff?' asked Simpson, hoisting
his club-foot on to a vacant chair, and passing his long,
bony fingers down the scar that runs vertically from his
forehead to his chin.

'I don't mind if I do,' I answered, and he gave me
another help.

I do not exactly know why I always dine with Simpson
on Christmas Day. Neither of us likes the other. He thinks
me a dreamer, and for some reason I never trust him,
though he is undoubtedly the most brilliant
Pantaeschrologist of his day, and we have been
contemporaries at the F.R.Z.S. It is possible that he dislikes
me, and I him, less than does anybody else. And to this may
be due our annual festivity in his luxurious rooms in
Gower Street.

'Have some of this sherry,' muttered Simpson, pushing
towards me a decanter which his deformed butler had placed
before him. 'You'll find it middling.'

I helped myself to a glass and smoothing out my shirt-
front (Simpson is one of those men who 'dress'), settled
myself in my chair.

'Notice anything odd about that pudding?' he asked,
with a searching glance through his double-convex glasses.

'No,' I said simply, 'I thought it very good.'

A gleam of grim pleasure came out of his face. I knew
from this that the annual yarn was coming. Simpson is the
most enthralling talker I ever met, but somehow I always
go to sleep before he is half-way through. I did so the year
before, when he told me about 'The Carnivorous Mistletoe',
and the year before that, when he told me 'The Secret of
the Sinister Crackers', and another time, when his theme
was 'The Microbes in the Yule Log'. It vexed him very much
every time, and he pooh-poohed my excuses. I was
determined it should not occur again.

Christmas revels: a Victorian view of Tudor merry-making at Haddon
Hall in Derbyshire, by Joseph Nash. The tall figure of Bold Slasher rises
out of the throng

Cutting the Baddeley cake at Drury Lane on Twelfth Night 1899

The Mari Llwyd procession at a cottage door in Llangynwyd, Glamorgan, c. 1909

'I am glad you liked the pudding,' he said. 'Pardon my inhospitality in not keeping you company, while you ate. Tobacco is a good preventive against indigestion. You can light up.'

I did so.

'You have heard of fossilized substances?' Simpson began, in that rasping voice so familiar to his pupils at the S.V.P.

I nodded across my briar.

'Well,' he continued, 'it has always been a pet theory of mine that, just as a substance can, by the action of certain alkaloids operating in the course of time, become, to all purposes, metallic, so – you follow me – it can, in like manner, be restored to its previous condition. You have heard of plum-puddings being kept for twenty-one years?'

I nodded; less, I am afraid, in assent than owing to a physical cause.

'Well,' I heard him saying, 'the stuff that you have eaten tonight is about two hundred and fifty years old and may be much more than that, at a very moderate computation.'

I started. Simpson had raised his voice rather suddenly. He took my start for surprise and continued wagging his crippled forefinger at me, 'That pudding was originally a cannon-ball. It was picked up on the field of Naseby. Never mind how I came by it. It has been under treatment in my laboratory for the last ten years.'

'Ten years,' I muttered. 'Ten . . . seems almost impossible.'

'For ten years,' he resumed, 'I have been testing, acidizing . . . thing began to decompose under my very . . . at length . . . Now comes in the curious part of the . . .'

How long after I don't know, I was awoken by a vicious kick from Simpson's club-foot. 'You brute!' I cried, 'you drugged that sherry!'

'Faugh!' he sneered, 'you say that every year!'

Max Beerbohm *The Saturday Review* **1896**

Mince Pies

After Christmas pudding these days most of us totter through to collapse in front of the Queen's speech. The English of the past were made of stronger stuff. After Christmas pudding they would probably have had a dozen or so mince pies. Mince pies were not filled with the spiced jam that you get today; like the ancestor of the modern Christmas pudding they were made with real minced meat. A recipe of 1394 for a Christmas mince pie required these ingredients: one pheasant, one hare, one capon, two pigeons, two rabbits – the meat separated from bone and minced into a fine hash. The livers and hearts of all these animals were added, also two sheep's kidneys, little meat balls of beef and eggs and pickled mushrooms, salt, pepper, vinegar and various spices, and the broth in which all the bones were cooked. All this was ladled into a large pie crust and baked.

Up to the Reformation the traditional shape for a Christmas mince pie was oblong, to represent the crib; sometimes it had a pastry child on top, which upset the Puritans who thought it was superstitious idolatry and a typically Popish custom. When Oliver Cromwell forbade the celebrating of Christmas he also forbade the eating of mince pies. Christmas celebrations returned when Charles II was restored to the throne in 1660, but gone were the pastry Jesuses on the tops of the pies, whose shape was no longer oblong, but round.

It was said that whoever ate a mince pie every day from Christmas to Twelfth Night would have twelve happy months after – if he did not die in the attempt. It was also a custom to make a wish on the first bite of the first Christmas mince pie. Perhaps the most famous of all the Christmas pies was the one into which Jack Horner stuck his thumb:

> Little Jack Horner
> Sat in a corner,
> Eating his Christmas Pie;
> He put in his thumb,
> And pulled out a plum
> And said what a good boy am I.

The rhyme is said to have an historical explanation. Jack Horner was a steward to Richard Whiting, the last Abbot of Glastonbury. At the time of the Dissolution of the Monasteries, the Abbot, hoping to curry favour with Henry VIII and so avoid losing all his land and revenues, sent Jack Horner to London with a large Christmas pie as a gift. Packed under the pastry were the title deeds to twelve manors belonging to the monastery. On the journey up to London Jack Horner is said to have discovered the secret of the pie and extracted the title deeds to the manor of Mells, in Somerset, where he went to live after the dissolution of Glastonbury.

Christmas Crackers

Crackers, like turkey and Christmas pudding, are an essential part of Christmas today, but, unlike turkey and Christmas pudding, give small returns for the capital outlay. If they went off like a shotgun and showered small diamond rings, cuff-links, or savings certificates, if the mottoes were really mottoes and the paper crowns fitted, then perhaps the expense would be justified. But not for the usual Christmas cracker; a loose assemblage of coloured paper containing a silent 'bang', a paper hat which tears on being unravelled, and a very tiny, broken, plastic toy.

The Christmas cracker is not very old, dating back only to Queen Victoria's reign. The inventor was a pastry cook and confectioner named Tom Smith. Apparently, while on holiday in Paris he noticed in several shop windows the sugared almonds which the French called *dragées*, or *bonbons*, which were sold in twists of coloured paper. He returned to London and tried the idea out there, later adding the novelty of putting printed mottoes or riddles in with the sweets. These did not sell as well as he had hoped but one day, gazing into the fire, watching the logs crackling in the grate, he suddenly had the idea of putting in the bang. After various experiments he devised the tiny explosion caused by the friction of two chemically impregnated strips of cardboard being pulled.

Crackers were originally called 'cosaques'. The dictionary suggests this refers to Cossacks, and 'probably with reference to their irregular firing'. Cossacks, one assumes, were notable for their irregular firing because of the difficulty they must have had in re-loading a rifle at full gallop.

Tom Smith was extremely proud of his crackers and the company he formed advertised them in flowing prose:

> *Thomas Smith and Company have endeavoured by employing special artists to produce designs, the finest modern appliances to interpret their work, and combining Art with Amusement and Fun with Refinement, to raise the degenerate cosaque from its low state of gaudiness and vulgarity to one of elegance and good taste . . . the Mottoes, instead of the usual doggerel, are graceful and epigrammatic, having been specially written for Tom Smith's Crackers by well-known Authors, among whom may be mentioned the late Tom Hood Esq., Charles H. Ross Esq., Editor of* Judy, *Ernest Warren Esq., Author of* Four Flirts, Laughing Eyes *Etc. . .*

An example of an 1891 motto went:

> *The sweet crimson rose with its beautiful hue*
> *Is not half so deep as my passion for you.*
> *'Twill wither and fade, and no more will be seen*
> *But whilst my heart lives you will still be its queen!*

Tom Smith also put novelties in his crackers: 'Grotesque and Artistic Head Dresses, Masks, Puzzles, Games, Conundrums, Jewels, Toys, Bric-à-brac, Fans, Flowers, Tiny Treasures, Japanese Curiosities, Perfumery, Scientific and Musical Toys, and many other surprises.' It seems that modern crackers contain only the Bric-à-brac.

One of the largest Christmas crackers ever made was for a Victorian actor named Harry Payne, who was playing a clown in a pantomime at Drury Lane Theatre at the time. It was seven feet long and filled with a change of costume for the cast, and hundreds of smaller crackers to throw to the children in the audience.

Christmas Presents

There is no traditional time on Christmas Day for exchanging presents, though Santa's stocking is usually opened first thing on Christmas morning. The ritual of the Christmas stocking is one of the more exacting responsibilities of being a father. To begin with there is little problem. During a child's earliest years, a change of nappies and some minced-up turkey and that's its Christmas. It is when it goes to school and hears Teacher talking about Father Christmas that the trouble begins. It wants to know where Father Christmas has been for the first five Christmases of its life. It will demand that Father Christmas should visit that year. This is the moment to go out and buy the red dressing-gown and the cotton wool. These should be put on, plus a pair of gumboots, before tiptoeing into the child's room to suffer the ignominy of hearing 'When is Father Christmas going to come, Daddy?'

The idea of giving presents goes back to the Romans. Presents called *strenae* were exchanged on the festival of the Kalends, which corresponded to 1 January. The high-ranking officials of the Imperial Administration were expected to present gifts to their Emperor. Caligula even presented an edict which stated that he *must* be given presents on the Kalends, and he stood at the porch of his palace on the day ready to receive them. Originally, these Kalends presents were only branches of evergreen picked from the grove of the goddess Strenia. Then the Romans gave gifts of honey and cakes that the New Year might be full of sweetness, and gold that the year might bring prosperity. Later still their presents became even more lavish.

The 'Kriss Kringle' legends of the Continent, that the infant Jesus himself delivered presents, helped to fix Christmas Day as the occasion for Christians to exchange gifts. At first, presents were very modest: a little money, cakes, apples, nuts, dolls, small toys, useful things like clothes and improving things like Bibles, writing materials and alphabet books. These were the traditional Christmas presents of a child in the

Middle Ages, arranged in the stocking with an apple at the top and an orange at the toe and a new sixpence somewhere in between.

Christmas Games

After Christmas lunch, when most families today are watching television, the families of the Middle Ages would be dashing about playing Christmas games. Besides the fun of playing these games for their own sakes, the games must have helped to shake down one meal before the revellers started on the next. In Normandy, seventy years ago, they actually made a thing of this shaking-down process. In between courses everyone would stand up, hold hands, and dance round and round the table singing *'En sacant! En sacant'* a literal translation of which might be: 'Put it in the sack! Put it in the sack!'

Playing games at Christmas was traditional till the Puritans' ban in 1652. In fact it was the only time that the working population was allowed to play games. Henry VIII issued a proclamation forbidding them at any other time.

> *Artificer, or Craftsman of any handicraft or occupation, Husbandman, Apprentice, Labourer, Servant at husbandry, Journeyman, Servant of Artificer, Mariner, Fisherman, Waterman, or any Serving-man [to] play at Tables, Tennis, Dice, Cards, Bowls, Clash, Coyting, Logating or any other unlawful Game, out of Christmas, under pain of twenty shillings to be forfeit for every time; and in Christmas to play at any of the said Games in their Master's houses, or in their Master's presence.*

Because games were not allowed at any other time of the year there were numerous Christmas games. By tradition snap-dragon was played on Christmas Eve, but it was often played on Christmas Day, too. Raisins, currants and other dried fruit were heaped on to a shallow dish, brandy was poured on top of them, the lights were extinguished and the brandy set on fire. The idea was to snatch the fruit out of the flames, blow the flames out and eat the fruit. A traditional song which accompanied this practice.

> *Here he comes with flaming bowl,*
> *Don't be mean to take his toll,*
> *Snip! Snap! Dragon!*
>
> *Take care you don't take too much,*
> *Be not greedy in your clutch,*
> *Snip! Snap! Dragon!*

With his blue and lapping tongue
Many of you will be stung,
Snip! Snap! Dragon!

For he snaps at all that comes
Snatching at his feast of plums,
Snip! Snap! Dragon!

But Old Christmas makes him come,
Though he looks so fee! fa! fum!
Snip! Snap! Dragon!

Don't 'ee fear him, be but bold –
Out he goes, his flames are cold.
Snip! Snap! Dragon!

King Edward II enjoyed playing Cross and Pyle, which was a game similar to calling Heads or Tails but involved betting on which would turn up. On one occasion he had to borrow five shillings from the court barber to pay his losses. On another royal occasion a visitor to the court of Edward IV was taken by the King to 'the Queen's own chamber, where she and her ladies were playing at the marteaux; and some of her ladies were playing at closheys of ivory . . .' Marteaux was a game played with small balls, each a different colour; closheys was a form of ninepins; loggats was another game very much like it. Nowadays the ninepins are made of wood or plastic; loggats were made of bone. This is why Hamlet, in the gravedigger-scene, says 'Did these bones cost no more in the breeding, but to play at loggats with them?' Kayles, Closh and Dutch Pins were other names for variations of this same game.

Popular outdoor games, besides tilting and archery, which did not count because they were weapon-training, included Prisoner's Base, which Edward III had to prohibit in the Approaches to Westminster Palace because so many people played it there that they blocked the traffic going towards the Palace. Another game, Hot Cockles, was popularly believed to have first been played by the ancient Egyptians. One person was blindfolded and knelt with his head on the lap of someone sitting in a chair. He then put his hand in the small of his back, palm upwards, and called out 'Hot cockles, hot.' The other players then hit his hand while the chap kneeling tried to guess who had hit him. If he guessed correctly, then the person guessed had to get down on his knees or suffer a forfeit. A letter to Steele's paper, the *Spectator*, drew attention to some of the problems of playing Hot Cockles: 'I am a footman in a great family and am in love with the housemaid. We were all at hot cockles last night in the hall these holidays, when I lay down and was blinded, because she pulled off her shoe and hit me with the heel such a rap as almost broke my head to pieces. Pray, sir, was this love or spite?'

Hot Cockles seemed to have been popular with courting couples. The eighteenth-century playwright John Gay wrote

As at hot cockles once I laid me down
I felt the weighty hand of many a clown.
Buxoma gave a gentle tap and I
Quick rose and read soft mischief in her eye.

Hunt the Slipper, Forfeits, Blindman's Buff and Hoop and Hide, which is now called Hide and Seek, all these are games which are still played today. But there are many other traditional Christmas games which survive in name only; games like Post and Pair, Puss-in-the-Corner, Feed the Dove, Rowland Ho, Shoeing the Wild Mare, Steal the White Loaf, The Parson has Lost his Cloak – all those splendid-sounding games have disappeared. The last game of all on Christmas Day was Yawning for a Cheshire Cheese. Towards midnight everyone in the house sat round in a circle. Whoever then yawned the widest, the longest, and loudest, and also produced the greatest number of yawns, was presented with a Cheshire cheese.

And Christmas Day was over for another year.

THE MISTLETOE BOUGH

*Thomas Haynes Bayly was an immensely prolific writer of songs,
books and dramatic pieces, mostly either treating of love in a whimsical
way or portending doom to one or more of the parties involved, both styles
being highly esteemed during the early part of the nineteenth century.
In the following piece he gives a grave warning of the danger inherent
in playing Christmas games like hide-and-seek without adequate
supervision.*

The mistletoe hung in the castle hall,
The holly branch shone on the old oak wall;
And the baron's retainers were blithe and gay,
And keeping their Christmas holiday.
The baron beheld with a father's pride
His beautiful child, young Lovell's bride;
While she with her bright eyes seem'd to be
The star of the goodly company.

'I'm weary of dancing now;' she cried;
'Here tarry a moment – I'll hide – I'll hide!
And, Lovell, be sure thou'rt first to trace
The clue to my secret lurking place.'
Away she ran – and her friends began
Each tower to search, and each nook to scan;
And young Lovell cried, 'Oh where dost thou hide?
I'm lonesome without thee, my own dear bride.'

They sought her that night! and they sought her next day!
And they sought her in vain when a week pass'd away!
In the highest – and lowest – the loneliest spot,
Young Lovell sought wildly – but found her not.
And years flew by, and their grief at last
Was told as a sorrowful tale long past;
And when Lovell appeared, the children cried,
'See! the old man weeps for his fairy bride.'

At length an oak chest, that had long lain hid,
Was found in the castle – they raised the lid –
And a skeleton form lay mouldering there,
In the bridal wreath of that lady fair!
Oh! sad was her fate! – in sportive jest
She hid from her lord in the old oak chest.
It closed with a spring! – and, dreadful doom,
The bride lay clasp'd in her living tomb!

Thomas Haynes Bayly (1797-1839)

THE BACHELOR FOR WHOM
CHRISTMAS COMING
ONCE A YEAR WAS MORE THAN ENOUGH

Dear Punch, – I live in lodgings. I am one of those poor unfortunate helpless beings, called Bachelors, who are dependent for their wants and comforts upon the services of others. If I want the mustard, I have to ring half-a-dozen times for it; if I am waiting for my shaving water, I have to wander up and down the room for at least a quarter of an hour, with a soaped chin, before it makes its appearance.

But this system of delay, this extreme backwardness in attending to one's simplest calls, is invariably shown a thousand times more backward about Christmas time.

I am afraid to tell you what I have endured this Christmas. My persecutions have been such as to almost make me wish that Christmas were blotted out of the Calendar altogether.

I have never been called in the morning at the proper time. My breakfast has always been served an hour later than usual – and as for dinner, it has been with difficulty that I have been able to procure any at all!

This invasion of one's habits and comforts is most heart-rending; and the only excuse I have been able to receive to my repeated remonstrances has been, 'Oh, Sir, you must really make some allowances; pray recollect it is Christmas time.'

Last week I invited some friends to spend the evening with me – but I could give them neither tea, nor hot grog, nor supper, nor anything – because, 'Please, Sir, the servant has gone to the Pantomime – she's always allowed to go at Christmas time.'

Now, Sir, it seems to me that Christmas is, with a certain class of people, a privileged period of the year to commit all sorts of excesses, to evade their usual duties, and to jump altogether out of their customary avocations into others the very opposite of them. For myself, I am extremely glad that Christmas does come but once a year. I know I shall go, next December, to Constantinople, or Jerusalem, or the Minories, or some place where the savage customs I have described do not exist; for I would not endure another

Christmas in England for any amount of holly,
plum-pudding, or Christmas-boxes in the world.
I have the misfortune to remain, *Mr Punch,*
Your much-persecuted Servant,
'AN OLD BACHELOR'

A Letter to *Punch* **1853**

The Years that Christmas did not Come

Of all the festivals in the Christian calendar, Christmas was unique in
the way in which pagan and Christian customs, legends and traditions –
mistletoe and midnight mass, ivy and Christmas cards – were all
intermingled.

On the whole nobody bothered about this rather surprising marriage
of opposites, but there was friction from time to time. During the reign
of Elizabeth I, Puritans had attacked the paganism of the Lord of
Misrule, which mocked Church practices, but in the seventeenth
century the Puritans denounced both the pagan and the Christian
traditions of Christmas. The pagan bits they denounced simply because
they were pagan; the Christian bits because they believed that the
celebration of midnight mass was Popish and stank of Rome. The title
alone of one Puritan pamphlet ran: 'Christmas Day, the old Heathens'
Feasting Day in honour to Saturn their Idol-God, the Papists' Massing
Day, taking to hearth the Heathenish customs, Popish superstitions,
ranting fashions, fearful provocations, horrible abominations com-
mitted against the Lord, and his Christ on that day and dayes
following.'

The Puritans decided to do away with Christmas altogether. The act of 1652 which abolished Christmas read: *No observation shall be had of the five-and-twentieth day of December, commonly called Christmas Day; nor any solemnity used or exercised in churches upon that day in respect thereof.* A war of pamphlets followed. One pro-Christmas pamphlet was entitled *A Ha! Christmas, This book is a sound and good persuasion for Gentlemen, and all wealthy men, to keepe a good Christmas. Here is proved the cause of Free-Will Offerings, and to be liberall to the poore, here is sound and good arguments for it, taken and proven out of Scripture, as hath been written a long time.*

But the Puritan cause had the upper hand, and there were no Christmas masses or festivities of any sort for eight years; at least not in public. John Evelyn wrote in his diary for 25 December 1656: 'I went to London, to receive The Blessed Communion this holy festival at Dr Wild's lodgings, where I rejoiced to find so full an assembly of devout and sober Christians.' The population were forced to worship behind closed doors and show no sign of the Christmas spirit.

A sympathizer wrote: 'The scholars come into the hall, where their hungry stomacks had thought to have found good brawne and Christmas pie, roast-beef and plum-porridge. But no matter. Away, ye profane! These are superstitious meats; your stomacks must be fed with sound doctrine.'

In 1660 back came the monarchy and back came Christmas. It may not have been celebrated with quite the same lavishness, but it was, to a great many people, a welcome return:

> *These holidays we'll briskly drink*
> *All mirth we will devise,*
> *No Treason we will speak or think;*
> *Then bring up the brave minc'd pies,*
> *Roast Beef and brave Plum-porridge,*
> *Our Loyal hearts to chear,*
> *Then prithee make no more ado,*
> *But bring up Christmas beer.*

CHAPTER VIII

26 DECEMBER,

BOXING DAY

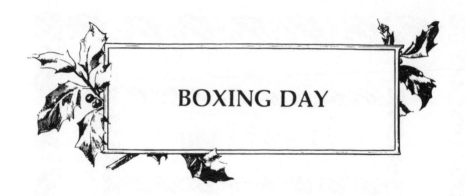

BOXING DAY

Christmas Boxes

B OXING DAY was probably named after an old Christmas tradition of placing alms boxes around the church over the Christmas period; these alms boxes were opened on Christmas Day itself and their contents distributed the day after. This traditional practice was called 'the dole of the Christmas Box' or 'the Box money'.

An alternative derivation was the long-established custom of apprentices and servants being allowed to ask their master and their master's customers for small amounts of money at Christmas time. This money they would collect in small earthenware boxes. Unlike modern piggy-banks, these earthenware boxes did not have a stopper in the bottom to get the money out and they had to be broken open. The apprentices therefore waited till the Christmas holiday was over and their boxes were likely to be at their fullest before breaking them open. This generally took place the day after Christmas – Boxing Day.

A rather later tradition, and one which has survived to this day, was the distribution of Christmas 'boxes', gifts of money, to those people who had provided services throughout the year; postmen, lamp-lighters, parish beadles, parish watchmen, dustmen and turncocks (the waterworks officials who turned the water supplies on), etc. Nowadays this money is usually handed over during the week before Christmas, but originally those to be tipped turned up on Boxing Day.

THE CHRISTMAS BOX NUISANCE

How much longer, we ask with indignant sorrow, is the humbug of Boxing Day to be kept up for the sake of draining the pockets of struggling tradesmen, and strewing the streets of the metropolis with fuzzy beadles, muzzy dustmen, and intoxicated – but constant – scavengers? We have received the usual intimation from our pertinacious friend who eases us of our dust, that he expects us to come down with our dust in another sense, at what the fellow sarcastically calls 'this festive season'. The gentleman who boasts of his constancy in scavenging has apprised us, according to his annual custom, that we are to ascertain his genuineness by a dog with a black eye, a white nose, a red ear, an absent tail, a swelling on his left cheek, and other little symptoms of his having lived the life of a busy dog rather than of a particularly lucky one.

The Christmas Box system is, in fact, a piece of horribly internecine strife between cooks and butchers' boys, lamp-lighters, beadles, and all classes of society, tugging at each other's pockets for the sake of what can be got under the pretext of seasonable benevolence. Our cooks bully our butchers for the annual box, and our butchers take it out of us in the course of the year by tacking false tails on to our saddles of mutton, adding false feet to our legs of lamb, and chousing us with large lumps of chump in our chops, for the purpose of adding to our bills by giving undue weight to our viands. *Punch* has resolved on the overthrow of the Boxing system, and down it will go before 1849 has expired.

Punch **1849**

St Stephen

26 December is also the feast of St Stephen, the first Christian martyr, who died for the new faith soon after Christ himself, perhaps even within the year. Although his life is fairly well documented, for example in the Acts of the Apostles, the popular imagination of medieval England fleshed out the bare facts of St Stephen's life, as it had the lives of both St Nicholas and Good King Wenceslas, and the result was a large number of intriguing legends.

A carol written in 1400 suggested that Stephen worked in the kitchens of King Herod.

> *Stephen out of kitchen came, with Boar's head in hand;*
> *He saw a star was fair and bright over Bethlemen stand.*
> *He cast down the Boar's head, and went into the hall:*
> *I forsake thee, King Herod, and thy workes all;*
> *There is a Child of Bethlehem born is better than us all.*

There was also another St Stephen, a ninth-century Swedish missionary whose name was connected with horses, as Nicholas's was with children. In fact, the feast day of the Swedish St Stephen was nowhere near Christmas, but his horses became part of the other St Stephen's feast-day celebrations in Europe. In England the horses were bled to give them good health during the following year. The same custom was observed in Austria, except that once a horse had been bled it was fed consecrated oats, salt, barley or bread.

In Munich there were services held on St Stephen's Day, during which two hundred men on horseback would ride horses decorated with coloured ribbons three times round the interior of the church. The Swedes used to take their horses at one o'clock on the morning of St Stephen's day to the banks of a north-flowing river and there let them drink, in order to ensure that they remained healthy all the year round. In the centuries before the motor car, these horse-blessing customs must have been very important to those who relied on horses both as agricultural machinery and as fast transport. Perhaps the present-day tradition of the Boxing Day hunt has its origins in the medieval celebrations of St Stephen's Day.

Costume design by Inigo Jones for *The Masque of Queens* by Ben
Jonson produced at the court of James I and Anne of Denmark
in 1609

Advertisement for a pantomime featuring Harlequin, placed in the
London Daily Post for 27 December 1742

First footing at Hogmanay in Scotland in 1882

Wren Hunting

In many parts of England, but particularly in Ireland and Wales, a popular Christmas sport was hunting and capturing the wren. The reason why this tiny, harmless bird should be chosen as quarry lies buried in several legends.

The Druids were popularly believed to have prophesied the future from the varying notes of the wren's song. To do this they had first of all to capture it. After the Druids disappeared, people continued to hunt the wren, though they had long forgotten how to prophesy the future. When the bird had been successfully hunted and captured, it was either put into a stable lantern or into a specially prepared 'wren house', which was a box painted to resemble a house with little doors and windows. With the wren in residence, the 'wren house' was paraded round the village or town in triumph by its captors.

Sometimes the wren was killed. This may have had something to do with the Christmas spirit of topsy-turveydom, e.g. the reign of the Lord of Misrule. During the year the wren was the king of the birds. He was greater even than the eagle because, though the eagle could fly higher than all the other birds, a wren once perched on an eagle's head and thus flew even higher. Once a year, though, the king of the birds was hunted and killed, perhaps to show how all rules were up-ended at Christmas time.

Another theory is that the wren was killed because it was supposed to have been the bird whose singing gave St Stephen away. How this could be believed when little else is known about the man suggests that it was probably an excuse dreamt up long after wren hunting had begun. Nevertheless there is an Irish rhyme:

> The wren, the king of all the birds,
> Was caught on St Stephen's day in the furze.

The Irish explanation for the wren hunt maintained that during the rebellion in the North a group of English soldiers were being surrounded while they lay asleep, but they were awoken by wrens pecking on their drums and managed to escape. For this reason the wren was called 'the Devil's bird' in Ireland and has been hunted ever since.

On the Isle of Man the explanation given for wren hunting was that a siren of the sea, who had been luring sailors to their death by her singing, only escaped her avengers by turning into a wren. There, the wren hunt could only end when the wren had been killed. The feathers of the dead bird were kept as a charm against shipwreck.

In parts of England too, where the wren hunt ended in the death of the bird, the tiny cadaver was hung on a branch of holly and carried to a mock funeral by the 'droluns' or 'wren boys'.

Grey Mary or Mari Lwyd

This is a much happier Christmas custom, which originated in south Wales. Mari Lwyd - no connection with the music hall star - was the name given to the horse which was turned out of its stable to make room for the holy family and has ever since been searching for shelter.

To represent Mari Lwyd, a horse's skull was mounted on the end of a five-foot pole which was covered by a sheet. Bits of black cloth in the shape of ears were sewn onto the head and the skull itself was decorated with ribbons. Pieces of glass were fixed into the eye sockets. A man stood beneath the sheet and worked the jaw-bone of the horse so that it made a snapping sound. A procession formed at one end of the town or village with the Mari Lwyd at the head. When they reached a house, they banged on the door with a stick and sang verses of a song which those inside had to answer. When the inhabitants became too tired to continue, or forgot the words, the Mari Lwyd was let in and rewarded with money and something to drink.

Hodening

Hodening was the Kentish equivalent of the Mari Lwyd, except that the horse was called Grey Mary in the south, and was represented not by the skull of a horse but by a hobby-horse. Contributions were fed in through its mouth. There was a traditional hodening rhyme:

> Three jolly hodening boys
> Lately come from town,
> For apples and for money
> We search the country roun.

Once hodening was over, the skull of the Grey Mary was hung up in the stables to bring good luck to the horses in the year to come.

Christmas Masques and Pantomimes

Boxing Day was traditionally the beginning of the pantomime season, though performances nowadays usually begin long before Christmas; but pantomimes only date from the beginning of the eighteenth century. Before that, the nobility had its own sort of entertainment: the masque.

It is difficult to imagine what the early fourteenth-century masques were like, because there is nothing like them today. They were similar to the Mummers plays in that the performers were masked and dressed up, but the educated noblemen rejected the curious subject matter of the Mummers in favour of topics more suited to their tastes, such as English versions of the Romance stories of the French medieval troubadours. To begin with, this new entertainment kept the name of its predecessor, 'mummings' or 'disguisings', but by the sixteenth century the productions had come to be called 'masques'. Calling these entertainments by an Italian name might suggest that they were immensely sophisticated productions, but until the seventeenth century, when poets and playwrights began to write masques, they were expensive fusses about nothing.

The Tudor chronicler Hall described the first Italian-style masque which was held for Henry VIII's court at his Greenwich palace on Twelfth Night, 1512:

> On the daie of the Epiphanie at night the King with XI others wer disguised after the manner of Italie, called a maske, a thing not seen afore in England; thei were appareled in garment long and brode, wrought all in gold, with visers and cappes of gold; and after the banket doen, these maskers came in and with six gentlemen disguised in silke, bearing staffe torches, and desired the ladies to daunce: some were content, and some that new the fashion of it refused, because the thing was not commonly seen . . .

By the reign of Queen Mary the court masques were like firework displays, only with the nobility instead of fireworks: 'a masque of patrons of gallies like Venetian senators with galley-slaves for their torch-bearers. Among them were lions' heads, sixteen other head-pieces, made in quaint fashion for the Turkish Magistrates, as well as eight falchions for them, the sheaths covered with green velvet, and bullioned with copper.'

The form of the masque was perfected in the reign of James I, with Ben Jonson writing poetic masterpieces and the architect Inigo Jones designing the costumes and the stage settings. Unfortunately the audience and participants were often less sophisticated than Jonson's poetry and Jones's scenery. One masque ended with King James being led from the chamber to have a lie down, while the two ladies playing Hope and Faith 'were both sick and spewing in the lower hall'. Masques were never solely a Christmas tradition, there were many occasions on which they were performed, but Jonson did write one specifically for Christmas, *Christmas His Masque*, performed before the Court in 1616.

The masque effectively perished, along with the royalist cause that had sustained it, in the Civil War. When Charles II was restored to the throne of his father in 1660, the monarchy had suffered such a beating that masques, always extremely expensive, were simply not possible on

the scale of those mounted for the first two Stuarts, and the masque form ceased to exist.

The tradition of the Boxing Day pantomime is nothing like as old as the tradition of the Mummers play, the mystery play, or even the masque. In the early eighteenth century, which saw the beginnings of the Christmas pantomime as we know it, the panto was not exclusively a Christmas entertainment; nor was it exclusively for children, but almost the other way round.

One of the first Boxing Day pantomimes was *Harlequin Sorcerer*, which was produced by John Rich at the Lincoln's Inn Fields Theatre in 1717. What Rich did was to take a classical story, such as *Perseus and Andromeda*, and mix in with it the traditional figures of the Italian *commedia dell'arte*, Harlequin, Scaramouche, Pantaloon and Columbine, Punch and the others, and give them all lines to speak. Rich also introduced transformation scenes into pantomimes. The first pantomime with a transformation was *The Magician, or Harlequin the Director*. Rich started by turning cottages and huts into palaces and went on to change everything into something else, even men and women into stools. Wondrous theatrical effects such as these made the eighteenth-century pantomimes very popular with the audiences, to the fury of dramatic actors and producers. The actor David Garrick expressed his dislike in verse:

> . . . *They that in drama find no joys,*
> *But doat on mimicry and toys.*
> *Thus, when a dance is in my bill,*
> *Nobility my boxes fill;*
> *Or send three days before the time,*
> *To crowd a new-made pantomime.*

During the nineteenth century the *commedia dell'arte* characters were dropped one by one in favour of 'turns', as in the music hall. The sense of spectacle was kept and the productions were based upon popular children's tales, or at least tales fit for children, hence *Babes in the Wood*, *Cinderella*, *Aladdin* and *Little Red Riding Hood*.

Pantomime was almost destroyed by the Victorian music hall, and when it was revived this century it still bore traces of music hall influence. It brought with it, for example, the Dame we know in modern panto. Furthermore, the music hall influenced the shape of the pantomime itself. There had always been singing, but now plot and action were suspended in order that a popular star of the day might sing a topical song, juggle, slap up wallpaper, or perform some other entertaining turn.

THE GRIP OF IRON
by Frank Muir

*It would have been fitting at this point to have included the text and
music of a pantomime which I had written and which dear readers could
then have performed over the Christmas period. Two things militated
against it; I have never written a pantomime, and even if I had it would
have been as long as this book. But several years ago I wrote a kind of
pantomime-substitute for my village dramatic society, which I now append.*

*I had considered knocking up a panto for the Thorpe Players –
for that was indeed the name of my village society – but as the stage in the
village hall only holds eight people at most, and then all breathing in
at the same time, it meant that, say, 'Ali Baba and the Forty Thieves'
would have to be presented minus thirty-three of the cast. So I wrote them
a little melodrama which could be simply staged, with three fat parts
and one small part (every dramatic society has a keen young beginner).
On another occasion I played the part of Silas myself, a thoroughly
enjoyable experience except for one small technical detail, which I pass
on for the benefit of others attempting the role: do make sure that after
you have stuffed a cushion up your back to simulate Silas's hump it is
firmly anchored with sticky tape or something. Some of Silas's
fearfulness tends to evaporate if, like me, you fail to fix the hump and it
gently descends during your last, big scene to come to rest in the seat of
your trousers.*

[*The scene is a dingy, sinister room in the middle of the last century.
There are two doors at the back and a sort of counter projecting from the
wings at the right of stage. This has a large lever on the downstage
side of it, rather like the ones seen in a signal box. As the curtain rises we
see* LUCY *sitting miserably in the centre of the stage on a stool.* LUCY *is
dressed in rather ragged clothes, but is attractive.*]

LUCY:
Oh dear, how unhappy I am, cooped up all day in this dark
old house with hardly enough to eat. Why is my guardian
so cruel to me? Sometimes I think there is something evil
about him. Yes, *evil*. He leaves the house at all hours of
the day and night and I never see him come or go. I know
he is supposed to earn his living making chess sets, carving
little chess men and putting them in boxes for rich people
to buy. But, if that is so, why is he so *mysterious* about it?

NEWSBOY [*off, shouting*]:
Evening Echo! Evening Echo! Another murder in London's streets! The Grip of Iron strikes again! Evening paper!

LUCY:
Oh dear, *another* of those horrible murders.

[*The* NEWSBOY *puts his head round the door left. He carries a bundle of newspapers and a paper which reads 'The Grip of Iron Strikes Again'.*]

NEWSBOY:
Evening paper, Miss? Another lovely juicy murder. They say it's the Grip of Iron again.

LUCY:
I haven't any money to buy one of your papers.

NEWSBOY:
Oh, what a pity, this is a real *good* murder, this is. It's the Grip of Iron, they think.

LUCY:
What do you mean, 'The Grip of Iron'?

NEWSBOY:
Coo Miss, you ain't 'arf ignorant. The Grip of Iron is the name they've given to this murderer who goes round strangling people. He's struck again tonight. That's the fourth this week.

LUCY:
Oh, how horrible!

NEWSBOY:
I know, lovely in'nit!

LUCY:
And don't they know who he is?

NEWSBOY: Somebody did catch a glimpse of him once. Dressed all in black he was, and sort of stooping. They call him The Grip of Iron because of his strangling, see?
Well, I better be off now or he might get *me* next. Ta ta!

[*Exit* NEWSBOY, *whistling cheerfully.*]

LUCY:
Another murder and I'm all alone in the house. If only my guardian would return. I'm frightened. *What was that?* No, it was nothing. I'll go up to my attic and finish my crust of bread.

[*Exits, right. There is a moment's pause, then a thumping is heard. The door left is kicked open and through it comes* SILAS DOOM, LUCY'S *guardian.* SILAS *has straggly, long, grey hair, a hump, and a very heavy limp. He is dressed all in black and carries a body on his shoulders. He glances swiftly round and cackles.* SILAS *limps across the room with his burden and lowers the body on to the counter arrangement projecting from the wings, right. He turns towards the audience and cackles again.*]

SILAS [*laughs*]:
The Grip of Iron strikes again! [*Laughs again.*] Nobody knows that I, Silas Doom, am the mysterious strangler. Nobody knows. Except *you!* [*Laughs. He turns back to the body.*] Another victim for the furnace. Into the fire goes the body and out come pure white bones. Bones that I carve and whittle down to make my little chess men. [*Laughs.*] My beautiful chess men. [*To audience*] My chess pieces are the finest in the world, renowned for their exquisite craftsmanship, but little do the fine ladies and gentlemen know as they shift the pieces upon the chess board that the chess men were once – *women!*

[*He turns back to the body, parts his hands about a foot and measures off one leg as though with a foot rule.*]

SILAS:
A good specimen. I'll get two kings and a pawn from the shin bone, a castle and two bishops from the thigh bone. A good night's work indeed! [*Laughs.*]

[*He pulls the lever at the side of the counter, a flickering red spotlight shines on his face from the wing and the body is whisked off stage.* SILAS *recoils from the heat of the furnace, shielding his face with his raised arm. When the body is out of sight, he returns the lever back to its first position and the spotlight is switched off.*]

SILAS [*to audience*]:
Don't be afraid. What are we all but pawns in the game of life? Only *I* can make you a *bishop* . . . or a *king*. [*Laughs.*] But to work. I must attend to my ward Lucy. She has become too inquisitive of late. I must [*laughs*] polish her off.
[*He calls towards door, right.*] Lucy! Lucy my dear, come down a moment, will you? [*To audience.*] These wrists do their work well, these fingers know their task. I have a grip of iron. [*Laughs.*] But hush, she comes.

[*Enter* LUCY *from door, right. She cowers when she sees her guardian.*]

LUCY:
Oh please, sir. Please spare me another crust of
stale bread. I am so hungry and I just gave my last piece
to the sparrows.

SILAS:
Of course you shall have more bread, my dear.

LUCY:
Oh thank you, sir.

[*She comes downstage and looks over the heads of the audience.
During her next speech* SILAS *goes into a crouch, extending his hands
into claws and, with an evil expression on his face, creeps up on the
unsuspecting girl to strangle her.*]

LUCY:
Oh sir, as I was feeding the sparrows from my attic
window, I saw a most horrible sight. There was one little
sparrow there who was so pathetic, so thin and starved-
looking and sad that I threw him my last piece of crust.
Then as he pecked away, all unsuspecting, a great evil
black cat crept up behind him. Crept up closer and closer,
his black claws ready to pounce. 'Look out, little
sparrow,' I cried through the attic window. 'Look behind you!
Danger!' But the little sparrow didn't hear me. 'Look out,
little sparrow!' I cried. 'Those claws!' But closer still
crept the cat until with one last bound . . .

[*There is a loud knocking on the door.* SILAS *springs back and
assumes a normal look as* LUCY *turns.*]

LUCY:
Oh, there's someone at the door. I'll answer it.

[*She goes upstage to door left.*]

SILAS [*to audience*]:
Cheated of my prey this time. Next time I'll make sure.

[LUCY *opens the door and an elegantly dressed young gentleman enters.*]

SIR TOBY FELTHAM: ·
Is this the residence of Mr Silas Doom? I wish to purchase
a chess set.

LUCY:
Pray come in, sir.

SILAS [*to audience*]:
He is a well-proportioned young man. I think I will add him to my collection. [*Laughs.*] [*To* SIR TOBY.] Your humble servant, sir. Lucy my dear, will you go into the store room and fetch the best chess men you may find there. Hurry, child.

[*Exit* LUCY, *right.*]

SILAS [*to* SIR TOBY]:
You are a connoisseur of the game, m'lord?

SIR TOBY:
My name is Sir Toby Feltham and I have heard talk in the coffee houses of the excellence of your chess men.

[*He strolls elegantly across the stage, looking around him with interest.*]

SIR TOBY:
These are strange quarters for an artist. The light is surely hardly good enough for fine carving.

SILAS:
I am a poor man, m'lord.

SIR TOBY [*noticing counter on right of stage*]:
Hello, what's this?

SILAS [*to audience*]:
Does he suspect?

SIR TOBY [*looking at counter arrangement*]:
Iron doors, a lever. What is this, some engine?
Some mechanical device?

SILAS [*to audience*]:
Curiosity shall be his undoing.

[*He creeps up on* SIR TOBY, *arms outstretched, his fingers formed into claws.*]

SIR TOBY [*still examining machinery*]:
'Pon my word, you artist fellows work with strange equipment nowadays. What is this stain upon the board here? It looks like dark red paint. Could it be, I wonder . . .?

[*The door starts to open as* LUCY *comes in.* SILAS *hears it in time and pretends he is showing* SIR TOBY *the furnace.*]

SILAS:
It is the furnace I use for hardening the enamel paint for my figures. Ah, you have brought the chess men, my dear.

[LUCY *hands him the box.*]

LUCY:
Here, guardian.

[SIR TOBY *takes one look at the box full of figures.*]

SIR TOBY:
Trashy. Have you nothing better?

SILAS:
I have indeed, sir. I have just completed the finest set
I have ever carved. Each piece pure bone. [*Laughs.*] I pray you
wait here. I will fetch it myself.

[*Exit.*]

SIR TOBY:
So you are Mr Doom's ward? [*To audience*]
How beautiful she is! Little does she know how often I have
watched her feeding the birds from her attic window.

LUCY:
Yes, sir. I keep house for him. [*Aside to audience*] I feel so
strange. I go hot and cold. I may faint. Is it indigestion?
Or am I falling in love?

SIR TOBY:
What a pleasant summer's day it has been, to be sure! [*Aside*]
What am I talking about, it's pouring with rain!

LUCY:
It was sunny *last* Sunday too [*Aside*] What am I saying, it's
Wednesday today!

BOTH TOGETHER:
TOBY:
What I really meant to say was –
LUCY:
I was really thinking about –

[SIR TOBY *catches hold of* LUCY'S *arm.*]

SIR TOBY: Lucy, there is something you must know –

[*The door right opens and* SILAS *stands there with a box in his hands.*]

SILAS:
Your chess men, sir.

[SIR TOBY *drops* LUCY'S *arm rapidly.*]

SIR TOBY:
Deliver them to my lodgings this evening – 14, Berkeley Square.
[*Goes to door left.*]
Bring them yourself, Mr Doom, and we shall discuss a price. I bid you good day.
[*Exit* SIR TOBY.]

SILAS:
Curses! [*Aside to audience.*] I like this not, I smell mischief. I must polish off this interfering young jackanapes *now*!
[*To* LUCY.] I think I shall follow him and strike while the iron is hot. Do you go to the attic now and stay there and don't come down to this room for the next hour. Understand?

LUCY:
Yes, guardian.

[SILAS *goes off rapidly, door left.* LUCY *stands rather fearfully centre stage for a moment and then the door opens and* SIR TOBY *flits back into the room.*]

SIR TOBY:
Quick, there is not a moment to lose. You are in great danger!

LUCY:
I don't understand. My guardian has gone to look for you.

SIR TOBY:
Yes, he's looking for me all right! To get his fingers round my throat!

LUCY:
What are you saying?

SIR TOBY:
Your guardian, my dear, is the man they know as 'The Grip of Iron'.

[LUCY *totters and is about to faint.* SIR TOBY *catches her and holds her to him.*]

SIR TOBY:
Don't worry, Lucy. I am here to protect you.

LUCY:
But my guardian – the strangler!

SIR TOBY:
Yes and you are next on the list.

LUCY:
Me! But why me?

SIR TOBY:
Because, Lucy, you are not just a little waif. You are heiress
to a fortune. And he is after it!

LUCY:
So that's why he's kept me cooped up in the attic.

SIR TOBY:
Yes. But don't worry. I am match enough for his villainies.

LUCY:
You, Sir Toby?

SIR TOBY:
Yes. You see, I am not really Sir Toby Feltham, Baronet.
My real name is . . . Honest Jack Strangeways, Bow Street
Runner!

[SIR TOBY *releases* LUCY *and bows to the audience. Then goes back
and gets hold of* LUCY *again.*]

SIR TOBY:
A law enforcement officer in the service of His Britannic
Majesty, King George III.

[*He releases* LUCY *again and takes another bow, then goes back to* LUCY.]

LUCY:
But what are we to do, Honest Jack?

SIR TOBY:
First I must examine how this furnace works. I must
open it. If you hear footsteps, cry out to me. He must not
catch us unprepared.

[LUCY *goes over to the door left to keep guard.*]

LUCY:
I'm certain he won't be back yet.

[SIR TOBY *goes over to the counter and bends over to examine the
machine carefully.*]

SIR TOBY:
This lever seems to work a sort of mechanism which
probably draws something into the furnace. And then
I suppose the furnace doors close and open with this
chain thing here.

110

[*As he is talking the door left opens silently behind* LUCY *and* SILAS *appears. He sums up the situation at a glance and then creeps up behind* LUCY. *Before she has time to turn he claps a hand over her mouth. There is a moment's silent struggle and she swoons in a dead faint on the floor.* SIR TONY *is still bent over the lever examining it.*]

SIR TOBY:
The furnace is probably stoked on the other side of the wall or possibly from the room above it. It's devilishly clever. Very clever indeed. Don't forget to keep watch, little one. You say he won't be back but he's as crafty as a weasel and as silent as a fox.

[SILAS *is a yard from* SIR TOBY. LUCY *raises herself a little and cries out.*]

LUCY:
Look out!

[SIR TOBY *whips round and presses back against the counter as hands reach for his throat.*]

SILAS:
I've got you now. [*Laughs.*] The Grip of Iron has never failed yet.

SIR TOBY:
It will *this* time. You see, your evil machinations have not gone *wholly* unobserved by those whom you laboured to deceive!

[SIR TOBY *takes a small bow and resumes his position almost in* SILAS's *clutches.*]

SILAS:
We'll see!

[*He grasps* SIR TOBY *by the throat and they heave around.* SIR TOBY *makes no effort to dislodge the grip but leaves his arms at his sides.* SILAS *strains away as though trying to strangle* SIR TOBY *but nothing happens.* LUCY *gets up and tries to pull* SILAS *off, but still* SILAS *presses away at* SIR TOBY'S *throat with apparently no effect.*]

SILAS:
What is this? The Grip of Iron is . . . *failing*! It has never failed before!

TOBY:
Go on, press away, Mr Doom! [*Laughs.*]

SILAS:
It is having no effect on him. I have been *cheated, cheated . . .*
He wears . . . a collar . . . of *steel*!

LUCY [*to audience*]:
Oh, what a *brainy* Bow Street Runner!

[SILAS *stands back in horror and despair.*]

SIR TOBY:
Take that, you swine.

[SIR TOBY *steps forward and delivers a swift upper-cut.*
SILAS *collapses in a heap.*]

LUCY:
Have you killed him?

SIR TOBY [*rubbing his knuckles*]:
No, I didn't hit him very hard. He'll recover consciousness
in four or five days. Beloved!

[*He holds out his arms.* LUCY *runs into them.*]

LUCY:
Dear one!

[*They clasp each other for a moment and then separate and face the
audience, hand in hand.*]

SIR TOBY:
And so, good friends, once more Good has triumphed
over Evil.

LUCY:
True Love has found its mate.

SILAS [*from floor*]:
And may we wish you, everyone of you, a Very Merry
Christmas!

Curtain

CHAPTER IX

27 AND 28 DECEMBER,

ST JOHN'S DAY AND HOLY INNOCENTS DAY

ST JOHN'S DAY AND HOLY INNOCENTS DAY

The Twelve Days of Christmas

THE CHURCH's explanation of the Twelve Days of Christmas, of which Boxing Day was the first, was that they represented the coming of men to God. Advent, the weeks before Christmas, represented the coming of God to men. The culmination of the Twelve Days was the arrival of the Three Kings at Epiphany.

The origin of the famous song which lists what 'my true love gave to me' to celebrate the Twelve Days of Christmas is not known. There are many versions. Amongst the gifts 'my true love gave to me' in a Scottish version is an Arabian baboon. In another version from western France, almost all the gifts are food: 'One boneless stuffing, two breasts of veal, three joints of beef, four pig's trotters, five legs of mutton, six partridges with cabbage, seven spitted rabbits, eight plates of salad, nine dishes for a chapterful of canons, ten full casks, eleven bosomy maidens, and twelve musketeers with their swords.'

St John's Day

In England, there were no particular customs celebrated on St John's Day, but in Scotland, Daft Days Yule bread was made. The Daft Days were the days between Christmas and Hogmanay, and probably so called to emphasize the difference between them and the rest of the year, while the bread was a thin oatmeal with the sign of the cross marked on it.

In Germany, St John's Day was commemorated by the drinking of large quantities of wine which had been blessed by the local priest. The wine drunk on this day was meant to make the drinker pretty, handsome, healthy, famous, or whatever. In the Tyrol district of Austria, drinking the blessed wine prevented you from being struck by lightning. The reason for this was that St John supposedly had once drunk a cup of poison and had remained unharmed.

Holy Innocents Day or Childermas

Holy Innocents Day, in remembrance of Herod's slaughter of the children of Bethlehem, was traditionally an unlucky day. No work was begun, no fingernails or toenails cut, nor new clothes put on. If anything of importance was begun on this day it would never be finished, or it would come to an unhappy end. The coronation of Edward IV was planned originally for 28 December, but it was changed to another day in case it led to a disastrous reign.

Children in Gloucestershire were sometimes allowed to play in the church on Childermas and special services were held. In many churches it was the big day for the Boy Bishops, who would take all the services and preach a sermon. The practice ended in the reign of Henry VIII. He forbade their services and their solemn processions through the streets afterwards.

There were various customs connected with whipping on Holy Innocents Day. The supposed reasoning behind these was that they would remind people, especially children, of King Herod's great cruelty. In fact it is more likely to have been a Christianised version of the Roman custom at Lupercalia, the festival of the god of herdsmen, when men ran through the streets clouting their womenfolk with leather thongs to drive out the evil spirits that women supposedly housed within themselves. Herod's gruesome deed was also commemorated in some parishes in west Somerset and Hertfordshire with a peal of specially muffled bells on Holy Innocents Day, and special carols were sung throughout the country.

Another Innocent, though perhaps not Holy, was Mr Pooter, who ran into a spot more inexplicable bother.

HOLY INNOCENTS DAY WITH THE POOTERS

DECEMBER 28:

We were rather jolly at supper, and Daisy made herself
very agreeable, especially in the earlier part of the evening,
when she sang. At supper, however, she said: 'Can you make
tee-to-tums with bread?' and she commenced rolling
up pieces of bread, and twisting them round on the table.
I felt this to be bad manners, but of course said nothing.
Presently Daisy and Lupin, to my disgust, began throwing
bread-pills at each other. Frank followed suit, and so did
Cummings and Gowing, to my astonishment.

They then commenced throwing hard pieces of crust,
one piece catching me on the forehead, and making me blink.
I said: 'Steady, please; steady!' Frank jumped up and said:
'Tum, tum; then the band played.'

I did not know what this meant, but they all roared,
and continued the bread-battle. Gowing suddenly seized
all the parsley off the cold mutton, and threw it full in
my face. I looked daggers at Gowing, who replied: 'I say,
it's no good trying to look indignant with your hair full
of parsley.' I rose from the table, and insisted that a stop
should be put to this foolery at once. Frank Mutlar shouted:
'Time, gentlemen, please! time!' and turned out the gas,
leaving us in complete darkness.

I was feeling my way out of the room, when I suddenly
received a hard intentional punch at the back of my head.
I said loudly: 'Who did that?' There was no answer;
so I repeated the question, with the same result. I struck a
match, and lighted the gas. They were all talking and
laughing, so I kept my own counsel; but after they had gone
I said to Carrie: 'The person who sent me that insulting
post-card at Christmas was here to-night.'

George and Weedon Grossmith *Diary of a Nobody* **1894**

CHAPTER X

31 DECEMBER AND 1 JANUARY,

NEW YEAR'S EVE AND NEW YEAR'S DAY

NEW YEAR'S EVE AND NEW YEAR'S DAY

Hogmanay

BEFORE THE Gregorian calendar was introduced into Britain in 1752, the New Year officially began on 25 March. Nobody celebrated it then, instead they chose to celebrate it on 1 January, which was perhaps a hangover from the Romans who celebrated the *Kalendae Januarii* on this day.

Ever since the Reformation, the Scots have always celebrated New Year's Eve rather than Christmas. When the Protestant reformers first attacked the traditions of Christmas, the Scots took it to heart much more than the English. They cut back heavily on Christmas celebrations transferring them instead to the New Year. The English went on happily celebrating both Christmas and the New Year.

The Scottish word 'Hogmanay' is thought to derive from an old French phrase exclaimed on New Year's Day, which translated means 'to the mistletoe the New Year'. Those who favour this explanation point out that throughout the late Middle Ages and Tudor times France and Scotland were closely linked by 'the Auld Alliance'.

There are alternative explanations. In the Highlands the men performed an extraordinary rite. One of the company covered himself with the hide of a cow which had been slaughtered that winter and ran round the village chased by other villagers, who hit the cow-hide with sticks. As they circled the houses they demanded to be let in. The doors would be opened and the men given something to drink. The leader of the group would give the head of each household the 'breast-stripe' of a sheep, deer or goat, wrapped round the point of a stick. This 'breast-stripe' was a piece of skin removed from the animal without a knife. The head of the family would then put the piece of wood with the skin wrapped round it into the fire and the family would pass it from hand to hand, breathing in deeply so as to suck the smoke right down into their lungs. This was a talisman against evil spirits. The point of which story is that sometimes the smoking stick was called a 'Hogmanay'.

Another theory is that 'Hogmanay' was the name given to the cheese and oat cakes presented to children on New Year's Eve. The children used to process up and down the streets, all wrapped into one sheet like a Chinese dragon, calling out for Hogmanay at the doors of the houses and reciting a special rhyme:

Get up, goodwife, and shake your feathers,
And dinna think that we are beggars;
For we are bairns come out to play,
Get up and gie's our hogmanay.

In Scottish towns Hogmanay was very much a communal celebration. Everyone crowded into the streets or congregated at the traditional meeting places, like the market cross or the churchyard. Bonfires were lit, torches were waved and tar barrels burnt. In the northern fishing villages an old boat was ceremoniously set on fire. Towards the end of January in the Shetland Isles a boat is still burnt commemorating Up-Helly-Aa, which is Norse for 'end of the holiday', the end of the Viking Yuletide. All these customs were linked to celebrate the Old Year being burnt out before the new could begin. During these ceremonies the Scots enjoyed the traditional drink of Hogmanay, het pint; warm mild ale spiced with nutmeg and laced with whisky. This was carried into the streets in copper kettles so that the revellers could drink a toast to the New Year.

In Aberdeen the New Year was toasted by drinking sowens. This was a gruel made from the insides of bran and oats. The gruel was sweetened with honey or treacle and then, like everything else on Hogmanay, laced with whisky. First-footers used to carry buckets of sowens, which they splashed about the door jambs of those they first-footed.

Inside the house, Hogmanay was the time for putting everything in order before the New Year arrived. The whole house had to be swept and all the debts paid. Anything that had been borrowed had to be returned, clothes mended, clocks wound up, musical instruments tuned, pictures which hung crooked on the walls straightened, silver, brass and pewter polished, and the beds in the house made up with clean sheets. Then there was the special Hogmanay food to be prepared: oatcakes, cheeses, shortbread, black bun, treacle bannocks and ankersocks. Black bun was a rich cake made with dried fruit, almonds, spices, and brandy baked in pastry. Ankersocks were gingerbread loaves made with rye meal. Inside the house on Hogmanay the fire was piled up high; the bigger the flames, the greater the luck to come. Any stray dogs living on the premises on New Year's Eve were shown the door because they were thought to bring bad luck. This superstition was also held in Wales. Marie Trevelyan described the Welsh terror of the stray dog on New Year's Eve:

The Cwn Annwn are celebrated as spirit-hounds passing through the air in pursuit of objects of their malice, and their howling is regarded as an omen of death. These dogs have been variously described. Sometimes they appear as very small dogs, white as the drifted snow, with tiny ears quite rose coloured inside, and eyes that glitter like brilliant moonbeams. In some parts of Wales they are described as being black and very ugly, with huge red spots, or red in body, with large black patches like splashes of ink. The most terrible of these spirit-hounds are said to be of a blood red colour, and when seen are dripping with gore, while their eyes resemble balls of liquid fire. In some places they are known as small liver coloured dogs, all spots and spangles of red and white, or flame coloured.

On the stroke of midnight the head of the house opened the door wide until the last stroke of the church clock's bell had died away. The Old Year had been let out and the New Year let in. Sometimes the windows were also opened and household bells rung, trays bashed, and pots clanged. The idea behind this was that the horrendous noise would send any malevolent influences lurking in the dark corners of the rooms screeching out of the house.

Afterwards the windows were shut to stop the spirits slipping back in again and Auld Lang Syne was sung, more het pint drunk, and the family staggered off to bed. If they were not first-footed first.

First-Footing

First-footing was once familiar to everyone in Scotland, a large part of the north of England, and some parts of the south. At the stroke of midnight, as everyone was standing around the fire, tot of het pint in hand, a knock would come at the door. The door would be opened in silence and a red haired man would enter. In one outstretched hand he would be holding a small branch and in the other a piece of mistletoe. The stranger would then walk to the fire, put his branch into the flames and place his mistletoe on the mantelpiece. Finally, he would wish the family a happy New Year and in return be given wine or whisky and a piece of cake. A fairly clear-cut custom, one would think.

Yet the first-footing custom was fantastically complex. The first person over the threshold fixed the fortunes of the household for the year to come, and some personages were held to be unlucky. For example, all women. Families would often rig the sequence of events rather than let a woman poison the fortunes of the whole house. Fair hair or dark hair on the first-footer was also unlucky. In Northumberland, and on the Isle of Man, flat-footed first-footers were *persona non grata*; they should have insteps sufficiently arched so that 'water runs underneath'. The Scottish were sensitive to a bewilderingly large

Wassailing the fruit trees with cider punch in Devon in 1861

A Ha!
CHRISTMAS,

This Book of

CHRISTMAS is a found and good

perfwafion for Gentlemen, and all wealthy men,
to keepe a good *Chriftmas*.

Here is proved the caufe of Free-will Offerings, and
to be liberall to the poore, here is found and good
Arguments for it, taken and proved out
of Scripture, as any hath been
written a long time.

By, T. H.

LONDON,
Printed, for *R. L.* 1 6 4 7.

A seventeenth-century broadsheet campaigning for the celebration
of Christmas

THE

TRYAL

OF

Old Father *Chriſtmas,*

FOR

Encouraging his MAJESTY's Subjects
in Idleneſs, Gluttony, Drunkenneſs,
Gaming, Swearing, Rioting, and all
Manner of Extravagance and De-
bauchery.

At the Aſſizes held in the

CITY of PROFUSION,

BEFORE

The Lord Chief Juſtice CHURCHMAN, Mr.
Juſtice FEAST, Mr. Juſtice GAMBOL, and
ſeveral other his Majeſty's Juſtices of Oyer
and Terminer and Goal Delivery.

By JOSIAH KING.

LONDON:

Printed and Sold by T. BOREMAN near *Child's*
Coffee-Houſe, in St. *Paul's Church-yard* ; and Sold
likewiſe at his Shop at the *Cock* on *Ludgate-hill.*

M DCC XXXV.

A seventeenth-century broadsheet campaigning against
Christmas

The Vindication of

CHRISTMAS,

OR,

His Twelve Yeares Obſervations upon the
great and lamentable Tragedy between the King and Par-
liament; acted by General *Plunder*, and Major General *Tax*;
With his Exhortation to the people ; a deſcription of that
oppreſſing Ringworm called *Excize* ; and the manner how
our high and mighty Chriſtmas-Ale that formerly would
knock down *Hercules*, & trip up the heels of a Giant, ſtrook
into a deep Conſumption with a blow from *Weſtminſter*.

Keep out, you
come not here,

O Sir, I bring
good cheere.

Old Chriſtmas
welcome ; Do
not fear.

Imprinted at London for G. Horton, 1653.

An illuſtrated pamphlet of 1653 attacking the Puritan tax on Christmas
ale. The figure in the centre of the woodcut represents Old Christmas.

number of personal peculiarities in their first-footers, being wary of those who were lame, blind in one eye, had splayed feet, whose eyebrows met in the middle, or were suspected of having the Evil Eye. They were not to be immoral but yet not sanctimonious, nor mean, nor were they to be carrying a knife or anything sharp.

The worst possible first-footer would seem to have been a decrepit old woman uttering a curse, or a one-eyed immoral crone with bushy black eyebrows which met in the middle who stood on the doorstep with her flat feet at ninety degrees to each other waving a knife.

Were one to suffer the misfortune of being first-footed by one of those undesirables, certain prompt action could avert the bad luck. You could sprinkle salt on the fire or speak to the undesirable before it spoke to you, make the sign of the cross or throw the burning embers up the chimney. Once he or she had left, you could still save yourself by putting a red ember into a bowl of water; or you could provide comprehensive household insurance by tying a cross of rowan twigs with red thread and mounting it above the doorway through which the first-footer must pass.

Sometimes, instead of the branch and the mistletoe, the first-footer brought bread, salt and coal, symbolizing life, hospitality and warmth. In fishing communities he sometimes entered with a herring. He generally expected to kiss all the women under his bit of mistletoe.

A Frenchman visiting Edinburgh at Hogmanay found the first-footers altogether too much for his refined tastes:

Jan. 1, 1811. There is no sleeping the first night of the year at Edinburgh. About midnight, it is a received custom for the common people to give a kiss to any woman in the streets, on foot or in carriages. Few women expose themselves to this rude salutation. But the streets are full, notwithstanding, of unruly boys who knock at house doors, and make a noise all night. This is a little relic of the coarse manners of former times, which is still tolerated; and considering what this country was before its union with England, there is, perhaps, many a reason to be astonished at the advanced state of its police than otherwise.

During the eighteenth century, in the south of England where first-footing was not common, glasses would be raised just before midnight: 'To the Old Friend! Farewell! Farewell! Farewell!' and when the bells had rung midnight a toast was drunk: 'To the new Infant! Hip-hip-hoorah! Hip-hip-hoorah! Hip-hip-hoorah!' In some places, when all the toasts had been drunk, everyone marched off to the farmyard and the barns to wish all living creatures good luck in the coming year. They would keep themselves going by eating special triangular mince-pies called God cakes; the shape was symbolic of the Trinity.

The very last custom of all was for bachelors and spinsters. Before they went to sleep, they put nine holly leaves into a handkerchief, tied it with nine knots and then slept with it under their pillow. This would guarantee that they dreamt that night of their future husband or wife.

A HOGMANAY REMINISCENCE
by Frank Muir

We were first-footed for the first time last New Year's Eve.
My wife was asleep in bed, and I was celebrating the
New Year in the bath with a can of light ale. Suddenly
the hounds began to bay. I thought it was probably revellers
on the way home from the pub. Let slip the hounds, a few
superficial lacerations, and that would be that.
But then there was a burst of song, a banging on the door,
and a thin alien voice calling through the letterbox,
'Lut ma een, um a fairst-fooooter.' I was baffled. My wife,
cooler at these moments, explained, 'Let him in, he's a
first-footer.'

I padded down the stairs in my dressing-gown and
let him in. With great ceremony he threw his arms out
wide and strode off towards the drawing-room, holding
a tiny piece of coke in one hand and a ten-pence piece in
the other. He was small and visibly Scottish, kilt and all.
A sad expression came over his face when he saw we had
no blazing fire; just a radiator. 'Where shall a poot eat?'
he said, offering me the lump of coke and the ten-pence.
I pocketed the coin and put the bit of coke on the mantelpiece.

We were left facing each other, neither speaking, yet
both having the feeling that it was not all over. He seemed
a little flushed and was standing at a slight angle.
Then my wife came in. 'You will want your glass of whisky,'
she said to him. So that was it! I went through to the
larder and rummaged for a bottle of whisky. None. I tried
the kids' collections of miniature bottles, the last resort
of the housebound dipsomaniac. I found a tiny bottle,
half empty, and returned to our first-footer. Unfortunately,
on my way back through the drawing-room I left the
door open and the hounds rushed past me like a streak of
summer lightning and stuck their long ice-cold Afghan noses
up the kilt of the first-footer in the traditional Afghan
gesture of welcome.

The last thing we saw of our first-footer was his lean
figure legging it down the gravel, miniature bottle of whisky
held aloft, kilt a-swirl. Mind you, ours was the fourteenth
house he'd first-footed since midnight.

New Year's Day

It was once a custom to give presents on New Year's Day, and this still happens in many parts of France, Germany, Austria and Spain. It was a throw-back to the Roman celebration of New Year, when it was customary to give gifts. In England presents were given on New Year's Day up until the reign of James I, when the time for giving presents was changed to Christmas. The traditions and customs associated with New Year's Day were concerned with bringing good luck for the year to come.

Hardly had the spinsters gone to bed with their holly under their pillows than they had to be up again. Before dawn they collected their pails and hared off to the village pump or well in the hope of being the first to draw water. This bucket of water was called the cream, or the flower, and whichever spinster drew the flower would, without a doubt, be married to the handsomest bachelor in the district before the year was out. If the first person to the well was already married, she would wash her milking pail in the flower and then carry a pailful to her cows so that they would produce abundant milk throughout the year.

Another custom allowed children to dash about with a jug of newly-drawn water which they could sprinkle on anyone they met.

Here we bring new water
From the well so clear,
For to worship God with,
This happy New Year.
Sing levy-dew, sing levy-dew,
The water and the wine;
The seven bright gold wires
And the bugles they do shine.
Sing reign of Fair Maid,
With gold upon her toe –
Open you the West Door,
And turn the Old Year go:
Sing reign of Fair Maid,
With gold upon her chin –
Open you the East Door,
And let the New Year in.

Before breakfast in Scotland there was the saining ritual. Sometimes this was done the evening before, but what with all the clanging of pots, first-footers and general merriment, it was often easier to carry the saining over to the next morning. The main ingredient was 'magic water', or urine, probably human, which was collected the evening before, when the sun was setting. The house was decorated with holly, hazel and rowan. The next morning the 'magic water' was sprinkled on the doorposts, walls and occupants. The farmyard animals got off comparatively lightly; they were just dabbed with tar. After this had been done, everyone went back inside the house and shut all the windows and blocked up all the keyholes. Then branches of smouldering juniper were carried from room to room. The idea was to cough, sniff, snort and spit at the smoke, which cleared any illnesses or diseases which might have been lying dormant in the family's tubes. The juniper branches were then extinguished and everyone sat down to breakfast.

After breakfast on New Year's morning, the fun started again. It was thought to be possible to tell what the New Year held by analysing the first thing seen. To see a person of the opposite sex was lucky but to see a group of people heralded a death. An animal, if standing, walking, or with its head towards the observer, was lucky – but God help the man who saw an animal lying down with its tail towards him.

In the Highlands of Scotland, boys used to whip each other with holly because they believed that for every drop of blood drawn they would live one year. This must have been the most painful seasonal tradition of all. An equally unusual but painless New Year's Day custom was performed at Queen's College, Oxford. Each year the Bursar would present all members of the college with a threaded needle, saying at the same time 'take this and use thrift'. The significance of this was that the

French for 'needle and thread' – *aiguille et fil* – was a pun on the name of the founder of the college, Robert of Eglesfield, who called his foundation Queen's College in 1340 as a compliment to Queen Philippa, the wife of Edward III.

In 1972 New Year's Day was declared an official Bank Holiday. The unofficial holiday that large numbers of people used to take on 1 January before it was a Bank Holiday, may have been absenteeism caused by hangovers but belonged, in fact, to the ancient tradition of celebrating the full Twelve Days of Christmas.

CHAPTER XI

5 AND 6 JANUARY,

OLD CHRISTMAS EVE AND TWELFTH NIGHT

OLD CHRISTMAS EVE AND TWELFTH NIGHT

Old Christmas Eve

UNTIL THE time of Julius Caesar the Roman year was organized round the phases of the moon. For many reasons this was hopelessly inaccurate so, on the advice of his astronomers, Julius instituted a calendar centred round the sun. It was decreed that one year was to consist of three hundred and sixty-five and a quarter days, divided into twelve months; the month of Quintilius was renamed 'July' to commemorate the Julian reform. Unfortunately, despite the introduction of leap years, the Julian calendar overestimated the length of the year by eleven minutes fifteen seconds, which comes to one day every one hundred and twenty-eight years. By the sixteenth century the calendar was ten days out. In 1582 reforms instituted by Pope Gregory XIII lopped the eleven minutes fifteen seconds off the length of a year and deleted the spare ten days. This new Gregorian calendar was adopted throughout Catholic Europe.

Protestant Europe was not going to be told by the Pope what day it was so it kept to the old Julian calendar. This meant that London was a full ten days ahead of Paris. The English also kept 25 March as New Year's Day rather than 1 January. By the time England came round to adopting the Gregorian calendar, in the middle of the eighteenth century, England was eleven days ahead of the Continent. A Calendar Act was passed in 1751 which stated that in order to bring England into line, the day following 2 September 1752 was not to be called 3 September, but 14 September. Unfortunately, many people were not able to understand this simple manoeuvre and thought that the government had stolen eleven days of their lives. In some parts there were riots and shouts of 'give us back our eleven days!'

Before the calendar was reformed, England celebrated Christmas on the equivalent of 6 January by our modern, Gregorian, reckoning. Which is why 5 January is known as Old Christmas Eve.

Fruit Tree Wassailing

The principal tradition on the evening of Old Christmas Eve was the wassailing of fruit trees, but like almost every other tradition in this book, different parts of England celebrated the custom at different times and in different ways.

In the main fruit-growing counties of Kent, Devon, Somerset and Gloucestershire, everyone would descend on one particular house where a wassail bowl had been prepared. Then they would troop off into the orchard with the wassail bowl into which broken roasted apples had been dropped. The bowl was put down amongst the trees and each man drew a cupful of the wassail brew, drank, and threw the remains of the liquid on to the roots of the fruit tree. They would often bend down one of the branches of the tree as they did so. Sometimes a little cake and a small pile of salt were left in the crook of the tree 'for the robins'. When this had been done, shotguns loaded with powder were fired at the branches of the tree and everyone shouted at it, urging it to produce a good crop in the year to come.

In Surrey orchards, instead of firing guns into the branches of the trees, the farmer would whip the trunks to encourage a fine yield. A song would accompany this. In Gloucestershire it went like this:

> Blowe, blowe, bear well,
> Spring well in April,
> Every sprig and every spray
> Bear a bushel of apples against
> Next New Year's Day.

In Kent, like this:

> Stand fast, root, bear well, top;
> God send us a yowling crop,
> Every twig, apple big;
> Every bow, apples enow;
> Hats full, caps full, bushel bushel sacks full,
> And my pockets full too! Hooray!

And in Somerset like this:

> Apple tree, apple tree, I wassail thee
> To blow and to bear
> Hat-vulls, cap-vulls, dree bushel bag-vulls,
> And my pockets vull too, hip, hip, hurrah!

Once the song had been sung, the men would plod back to the farmhouse. There was one more game to be played. The women inside would not let the men in until they had guessed what kind of meat was cooking for their supper.

The Church, acknowledging the pagan need to celebrate kings, chose 6 January to commemorate the arrival of the Three Kings in Bethlehem. Another example of pagan customs being given a Christian connotation.

A ceremony takes place to this day in the Chapel Royal, St James's Palace, to commemorate the three gifts of the Three Kings. The reigning monarch processes in state to the chapel and presents gold, frankincense and myrrh to the officiating clergy, who hold out an alms dish. The monarch has been represented by two men from the Lord Chamberlain's office since George III's reign, when the King was judged too mad to cope with the ceremony himself.

Most of the customs associated with this day were a great deal more pagan and a good deal less magnificent. But then the Three Kings were only visitors.

JOURNEY OF THE MAGI

A cold coming we had of it
Just the worst time of the year
For a journey, and such a long journey:
The ways deep and the weather sharp,
The very dead of winter.
And the camels galled, sore-footed, refractory,
Lying down in the melted snow.
There were times we regretted
The summer palaces on slopes, the terraces,
And the silken girls bringing sherbet.
Then the camel men cursing and grumbling
And running away, and wanting their liquor and women,
And the night-fires going out, and the lack of shelters,
And the cities hostile and the towns unfriendly
And the villages dirty and demanding high prices:
A hard time we had of it.
At the end we preferred to travel all night,
Sleeping in snatches,
With the voices singing in our ears, saying
That this was all folly.

Then at dawn we came down to a temperate valley,
Wet, below the snow line, smelling of vegetation,
With a running stream and a water-mill beating the darkness,
And three trees on the low sky.
And an old white horse galloped away in the meadow.
Then we came to a tavern with vine-leaves over the lintel,
Six hands at an open door dicing for pieces of silver,
And feet kicking the empty wine-skins.
But there was no information, and so we continued
And arrived at evening, not a moment too soon
Finding the place; it was (you may say) satisfactory.

All this was a long time ago, I remember,
And I would do it again, but set down
This set down
This: were we led all that way for
Birth or Death? There was a Birth, certainly,
We had evidence and no doubt. I had seen birth and death,
But had thought they were different; this Birth was
Hard and bitter agony for us, like Death, our death.
We returned to our places, these Kingdoms,
But no longer at ease here, in the old dispensation,
With an alien people clutching their gods.
I should be glad of another death.

T. S. Eliot, 1927

The Twelfth Night Cake

On Twelfth Night in Herefordshire and Gloucestershire, the farmers would light twelve small bonfires and one large one in their main wheatfields. Then they would gather together with their farmhands and stand in a large circle toasting the harvest to come. This was thought to protect the wheat from disease. An Irish variation of this was to set up a sieve full of oats around which were placed twelve small candles and one large one. These were said to represent Christ and his twelve apostles as the lights of the world.

Twelfth Night is the traditional time for packing up Christmas decorations, felling the tree and sweeping up all the thousands of needles which always fall off. Failing to take down the Christmas decorations on Twelfth Night could mean bad luck for the rest of the year. The seventeenth-century poet Herrick maintained that decorations should be kept up right through till Candlemas, which is on 2 February. Then was the time to cry:

> Down with the Rosemary and Bayes,
> Down with the Mistletoe!

The Twelfth Night cake was baked in honour of the Three Kings but the traditions that went with it were pagan in origin. One method of selecting who was to play the King was to put a coin in the mix; the man who got the coin was the Twelfth Night King. The more popular way was to bury both a bean and a pea; the man who found the bean was King and the woman who found the pea was Queen. If a woman found the bean then she could choose her King; if a man found the pea then he was entitled to pick his Twelfth Night Queen. Herrick described the ritual in greater detail in his poem *Twelfe Night*.

Now, now the mirth comes
With the cake full of plums,
Where Beane's the King of the sport here;
Beside we must know,
The Pea also
Must revell, as Queene, in the court here.

Begin then to chuse,
(This night as ye use)
Who shall for the present delight here,
Be a King by the lot,
And who shall not
Be Twelfe-day Queen for the night here.

Whiche knowne, let us make
Joy-sops with the cake;

And let not a man then be seen here,
Who unurg'd will not drinke
To the base from the brink
A health to the King and the Queene here

Next crowne the bowle full
With gentle lambs-wooll;
Adde sugar, nutmeg and ginger,
With store of ale too;
And thus ye must doe
To make the wassaile a swinger.

Give them to the King
And Queene wassailing;
And though with ale he be whet here;
Yet part ye from hence,
As free from offence,
As when ye innocent met here.

In France the saying *'Il a trouvé la fève au gâteau'* – he has found a bean in his cake – refers to the Twelfth Night cake and is said of someone who has good luck. When Mary Queen of Scots had Twelfth Night cake at the palace of Holyrood in 1563, her maid Mary Fleming drew the bean and was dressed in the Queen's own clothes for the rest of the day.

In the nineteenth century you could buy special cards, which cake makers sold with their Twelfth Night cakes, and with these elect a whole court of characters to go with the Twelfth Night King and Queen. You put the cards in a hat, jumbled them about and then passed the hat around for everybody to pick out a character to play. To begin with, the characters were the worthies of history and the heroes of stories and legends, but by the time the tradition had died out specially invented characters had been introduced with names like Sir Tunbelly Clumsy and Sir Gregory Goose.

In 1795 a pastrycook turned actor called Robert Baddeley left a sum of money in his will which was to 'Provide cake and wine for the performers in the green room of Drury Lane Theatre on Twelfth Night'. The cutting of Baddeley's Cake continues to this day.

The village of Haxey in Lincolnshire celebrated Twelfth Night with the traditional game of Haxey Hood. This was a primitive form of rugger, the men of Haxey struggling against the men of Westwoodside for the possession of a roll of leather or sacking called 'the hood'; the game was refereed by a figure known as 'my Lord' who was attended by a fool. At the beginning of the game the fool made a speech of introduction, then six hoods were thrown up into the air. The winning team was the one that carried the greater number of hoods over the boundary.

The Glastonbury Thorn

It was once quite widely held, and still is by some people, that the man who introduced Christianity into Britain was Joseph of Arimathea; the same man who arranged for the burial of Jesus after the Crucifixion. Joseph of Arimathea landed on the Isle of Avalon and began walking. He was tired after his journey so lay down to sleep, but before he did so he stuck his staff into the ground. When he woke, he found that the staff had taken root. The resultant bush was the Glastonbury thorn, which flowered every year on Christmas Day.

An Elizabethan Puritan felled the original thorn because he thought it was blasphemous idolatry, but many cuttings had been taken by pilgrims and half a dozen thorns grew in different parts of the country. But there was a snag in watching for the Glastonbury thorns to bloom on Christmas Day; which Christmas Day? Since the calendar had been changed there were two. *The Gentleman's Magazine* in 1753 reported:

> Quainton in Buckinghamshire, Dec. 24. *Above 2000 came here this night, with lanthorns and candles, to view a blackthorn which grows in this neighbourhood, and which was remembered (this year only) to be a slip from the famous Glastonbury thorn that always budded on the 24th, and was full blown the next day, and went all off at night: but the people finding no appearance of a bud, 'twas agreed by all, that December 25 N.S. (New Style) could not be the right Christmas Day, and accordingly they refused to go to church, and treated their friends on that day as usual: at length the affair became so serious, that the ministers of the neighbouring villages, in order to appease the people, thought it prudent to give notice that the old Christmas Day should be kept holy as before.*

The dull botanical truth behind the legend of the Glastonbury thorn is that *Crataegus monogyna biflora*, its official name, flowers twice a year and generally one of these occasions is at Christmas time.

Joseph of Arimathea's staff is a much better story.

CHAPTER XII

DISTAFF DAY AND
PLOUGH MONDAY

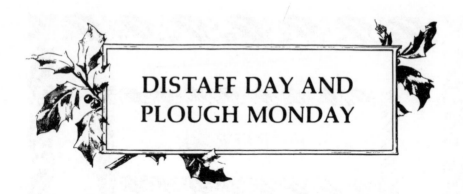

DISTAFF DAY AND PLOUGH MONDAY

WELL, SO THAT IS THAT

WELL, SO that is that. Now we must dismantle the tree,
 Putting the decorations back into their cardboard
boxes –
Some have got broken – and carrying them up into the attic.
The holly and the mistletoe must be taken down and burnt,
And the children got ready for school. These are enough
Left overs to do, warmed-up, for the rest of the week –
Not that we have much appetite, having drunk such a lot,
Stayed up so late, attempted – quite unsuccessfully –
To love all of our relatives, and in general
Grossly overestimated our powers. Once again
As in previous years we have seen the actual Vision and failed
To do more than entertain it as an agreeable
Possibility. Once again we have sent Him away,
Begging though to remain His disobedient servant,
The promising child who cannot keep His word for long.
The Christmas Feast is already a fading memory,
And already the mind begins to be vaguely aware
Of an unpleasant whiff of apprehension at the thought
Of Lent and Good Friday which cannot, after all, now
Be very far off. But, for the time being, here we all are,
Back in the moderate Aristotelian city
Of darning and the Eight-Fifteen, where Euclid's geometry
And Newton's mechanics would account for our experience,
And the kitchen table exists because I scrub it.

It seems to have shrunk during the holidays. The streets
Are much narrower than we remembered; we had forgotten
The office was as depressing as this. To those who have seen
The Child, however dimly, however incredulously
The Time Being is, in a sense, the most trying time of all.
For the innocent children who whispered so excitedly
Outside the locked door where they knew the presents to be
Grew up when it opened. Now, recollecting that moment
We can repress the joy, but the guilt remains conscious;
Remembering the stable where for once in our lives
Everything became a You and nothing was an It.
And craving the sensation but ignoring the cause,
We look round for something, no matter what, to inhibit
Our self-reflection, and the obvious thing for that purpose
Would be some great suffering. So, once we have met the Son,
We are tempted ever after to pray to the Father:
'Lead us not into temptation and evil for our sake'.
They will come all right, don't worry; probably in a form
That we do not expect, and certainly with a force
More dreadful than we can imagine. In the meantime
There are bills to be paid, machines to keep in repair,
Irregular verbs to learn, the Time Being to redeem
From insignificance. The happy morning is over,
The night of agony still to come; the time is noon:
When the Spirit must practise his scales of rejoicing
Without even a hostile audience, and the Soul endure
A silence that is neither for nor against her faith
That God's Will will be done, that, in spite of her prayers,
God will cheat no one, not even the world of its triumph.

W. H. Auden *For the Time Being* **1944**

Distaff Day

Distaff Day was traditionally the day when women went back to work after the Christmas festivities. The men went back on Plough Monday, the first Monday after Twelfth Night. Except for the years when Twelfth Night fell on a Sunday, this meant that men got a longer holiday than women.

Herrick wrote a poem for Distaff Day:

> *Partly worke and partly play*
> *Ye must on S. Distaffs day:*
> *From the Plough soone free your teame;*
> *Then come home and fother them.*
> *If the Maides a spinning goe,*
> *Burne the flax, and fire the tow:*
> *Scorch their plackets, but beware*
> *That ye singe no maiden-haire.*
> *Bring in pailes of water then,*
> *Let the Maides bewash the men.*
> *Give S. Distaffe all the right,*
> *Then bid Christmas sport good-night.*
> *And next morrow, every one*
> *To his owne vocation.*

In Herrick's part of the country, Devon, the men seem to have gone back to work on Distaff Day with the women; neither for very long, though.

Plough Monday

People were far too busy celebrating the return to work on Plough Monday to do much ploughing. Work was taken more seriously on the Tuesday. All the young labourers would rise before dawn because the one who could get his plough staff, hatchet or whip beside the farmhouse fireplace before the kettle had been put on won the promise of a cockerel at Shrovetide. Next, all the farm labourers gathered at a particular spot on the outskirts of the village. They left off their jackets and wore clean shirts, with ribbon bows sewn on to the elbows and shoulders. They also wore ribbons in their hats. Two of them were dressed differently, these were the Bess or Betsy, and the Fool. The Betsy was a boy dressed up with a tall hat and a false nose. The Fool dressed in skins and waved an inflated bladder. The labourers lined up behind a beribboned plough, all holding on to a length of rope fixed to the stilts of the plough. The leader took hold of these and the procession moved off through the village. Much shouting and cheering accompanied the plough, with the Fool cavorting about and the Betsy collecting money. The money went to maintaining a Plough Light in the church; if this light should ever go out, dark days were prophesied for the village and its crops.

Sometimes the plough procession ended with a sword dance. The Fool knelt down and the dancers locked their swords over his head. With a shout, the dancers pulled their swords away and the Fool keeled over as if dead. In the Lincolnshire Revesby Play, it is the Fool's five sons who kill him:

> *Good people all, you see what we have done;*
> *We have cut our father down like the evening sun,*
> *And here he lies all in his purple gore,*
> *And we are afraid he will never dance more.*

But then the Fool is on his feet again:

> *No, no my children; by chance you are all mista'en,*
> *For here I find myself, I am not slain:*
> *But I will rise, your sport for to advance,*
> *And with you all, brave boys, I'll have a dance.*

The Sword Dance appears to have elements of a pagan ritual murder, and of Christ's crucifixion. The Betsy has been interpreted as a caricature of Freyia, the Norseman's Venus, but the words of the Fool and his five sons in the Revesby Play equally express the mood of the end of the Christmas holidays. Each year the spirit of Christmas is summoned up, is celebrated and dies again.

Despite the dreadfulness of much of our modern commercialized celebrations, the spirit of Christmas still seems to say, like the Revesby Fool:

> *. . . I am not slain:*
> *But I will rise, your sport for to advance,*
> *And with you all . . . I'll have a dance.*

INDEX

Advent, 114
Albert, Prince, 65
All Hallows Eve, 10, 19ff.
Anatomie of Abuses, 21
Annunciation of the Virgin, 14
Arthur of Britain, 52
Auden, W.H., 9, 138-9
Auld Lang Syne, 120

Baddeley, Robert, 134
Baron's Yule Feast, The, 59-60
Bayley, Thomas Haynes, 88-9
Bede, Venerable, 15
Beerbohm, Max, 80-1
Bennett, C.H., 34
Betjeman, Sir John, 16-17
Boar's Head Feast, 52-3
Boxing Day, 93ff.
Boxing Day Hunt, 96
Boy Bishops, 42-3, 115
Bradley, Reverend Edward, 33
Brillat-Savarin, J.A., 78
Brumalia, 14

Cabot, Sebastian, 78
Caesar, Julius, 128
cake, Christmas, 32-3
Calendar Act of 1751, 128
Caligula, 84
candles, 74
cards, 33ff.
Chadlington, 25
Chapel Royal, 130
Charlemagne, 78
Charles I, 51
Charles II, 21, 82, 100
Childermas, 115
Christmas, 16-17
Christmas boxes, 94-5
Christmas Card Artillery, The, 35-7
Christmas Carol, A, 34
Christmas Eve, 58ff.
Christmas His Masque, 100
Christmas stocking, 84
Christmas tree, 64-6
Christmas Tree in Household Words, A, 66
Clare, John, 44ff.
Cole, Sir Henry, 33

Connor, William, 35-7, 79
Constantine, Emperor, 14
Cooper, Thomas, 59
crackers, 83-4
crib, 67-8
Cromwell, Oliver, 82
Culhwch and Olwen, 52

Daft Days, 114
decorations, 62-3
Diary of a Nobody, The, 54-5, 77, 116
Dickens, Charles, 9, 13, 34, 66
Distaff Day, 137ff.
Dobson, W.C.T., 33
Druids, 63, 97
Dumb Cake, 61-2

Edward I, 42
Edward II, 86
Edward III, 20, 86, 124
Edward IV, 86, 115
Eglesfield, Robert of, 124
Egley, William Maw, 33
Eliot, T.S., 131-2
Elizabeth I, 21, 43, 91
English Festivals, The, 67
Epiphany, 114, 133-4
Evelyn, John, 92

Father Christmas, 23, 41
Feast of Fools, The, 20
Feast of Lights (Hanuca), 14, 74
Feast of St Nicholas, 39ff.
Feast of the Circumcision, 20
first-footing, 9, 120ff.
Fleming, Mary, 134
food, Christmas, 76
For the Time Being, 138-9
fruit tree wassailing, 129-30

games, 85ff.
Garrick, David, 102
Gay, John, 87
Gentleman's Magazine, The, 135
George III, 130
Glastonbury Thorn, 135
Good King Wenceslas, 43, 96
Gregorian Calendar, 128

Gregory XIII, Pope, 128
Greville, Charles, 65
Grip of Iron, The, 103ff.
Grossmith, George and Weedon, 54-5, 77, 116

Hakon the Good, King, 15
Hall, 100
Hamlet, 73, 86
Hanuca, 14, 74
Hardy, Thomas, 24, 72-3
Harlequin Sorcerer, 102
Haxey Hood, 124
Henry V, 76
Henry VIII, 22, 42, 76, 82, 85, 100, 115
Herod, 96, 115
Herrick, Robert, 58, 133, 140
hodening, 99
Hogmanay, 74, 114, 118ff.
Holy Innocents Day, 113ff.
Horner, Jack, 82
Horsley, John, 33

Jacob, Georg, 64
James I, 43, 100, 123
Jones, Inigo, 100
Jonson, Ben, 100
Joseph of Arimathea, 135
Journey of the Magi, 131-2
Julian calendar, 128
Juvenalia, 14

Kalendae Januarii, 14, 118
Kalends, 84
Kilvert, Reverend Francis, 61, 75
Kissing Bough, 67
'Kriss Kringle', 41, 84

Lamb, Charles, 79
Lieven, Princess, 65
Lord of Misrule, 20-21, 91, 97
Lupercalia, 115
Luther, Martin, 64

Magician, The, 102
Mari Lwyd (Grey Mary), 99
Mary Tudor, 43, 100
Mary, Queen of Scots, 134
masques, 99ff.
Massinger, Philip, 76
midnight mass, 72, 91
mince pies, 82
mistletoe, 51, 63-4, 91
Mistletoe Bough, The, 88-9
Mithras, 14

Moore, Clement Clarke, 41, 69-70
Mummers, 22-4, 100, 102
Mummers Play, A, 25ff.
music hall, 102

Nast, Thomas, 41
Nativity, 14, 59, 73
New Year's Day, 123-5
New Year's Eve, 117ff.
Norsemen, 15, 41

Old Christmas Eve, 127-8
Old Lad's Passing Bell, 68

pantomime, 99ff.
Payne, Harry, 84
Plough Monday, 10, 140-41
plum pudding, 32, 79, 80-81
Pooter, Mr, 54-5, 77, 115, 116
presents, 84-5
Punch, 54, 90-91, 95
Puritans, 21, 82, 85, 91-2

Queen's College, Oxford, 52, 124

Return of the Native, The, 24
Revesby Play, 141
Rich, John, 102
Romans, 14, 20, 40, 62, 78, 84, 115, 123, 128

saining, 124
St Augustine, 15
St Bonaventure, 67-8
St Boniface, 64
St Francis of Assisi, 67
St George, 23
St Gregory, 15
St John, 113ff.
St Luke, 14
St Matthew, 14
St Nicholas, 9, 39ff., 69-70, 96
St Stephen, 96
St Thomas, 49ff.
Santa Claus, 9, 41-2, 84
Saturn, 14, 91
Saturnalia, 14, 20, 41
Shakespeare, William, 73
Shepherd's Calendar, The, 44ff.
Sketches by Boz, 12-13
Skinner, John, 73-4
Smith, Tom, 83-4
sowen cakes, 74
Steele, Richard, 63, 86
Stir Up Sunday, 31ff., 79

Strype, John, 42
Stubbes, Philip, 21

Tertullian, 15
Thomasing, 50
Thor, 59
Three Kings, 114, 130
Treatise of Idolatry, 15
Trevelyan, Marie, 119-20
turkey, 78-9
Twelfe Night, 133-4
Twelfth Night, 133-4
Twelfth Night cake, 32, 133-4
Twelve Days of Christmas, 114, 125

Up-Helly-Aa, 119

Victoria, Queen, 33, 65, 83
Visit from St Nicholas, A, 69-70

wassailing, 51-2, 129-30
Whistler, Laurence, 67
Whiting, Richard, 82
Woden, 41
wren hunting, 97ff.

Yule, 15
Yule log, 58-60, 62